The Legends of Genesis.

The Legends of Genesis

THE BIBLICAL SAGA AND HISTORY

HERMANN GUNKEL

Introduction by
WILLIAM F. ALBRIGHT

SCHOCKEN BOOKS • *NEW YORK*

Translated by W. H. Carruth.
First published in 1901.

First SCHOCKEN PAPERBACK *edition 1964*

Copyright © 1964 Schocken Books, Inc.
Library of Congress Catalog Card No. 64-22609
Manufactured in the United States of America

CONTENTS

INTRODUCTION

HERMANN GUNKEL was one of the most remarkable Old Testament scholars of modern times. Born in May, 1862, and deceased in March, 1932, shortly before his seventieth birthday, he was considerably younger than Julius Wellhausen. The influence of Wellhausen, however, was so pervasive in the late nineteenth and early twentieth centuries that it was left for our own day to fully appreciate the great originality of Gunkel's scholarship. By 1895 Gunkel had published *Creation and Chaos,* followed in 1901 by his still more famous *Commentary on Genesis,* which was introduced by the survey here reprinted in translation.

The approach of Wellhausen to Israelite literature was essentially isolationist; he refused to recognize the antiquity of oral tradition and insisted that the stories of Genesis were, in general, reflections of life and religion in the period of the Monarchy, erroneously projected backward into pre-Mosaic times. According to Wellhausen the ancient Orient, with its foci in Egypt and Mesopotamia, exerted no serious influence on early Israel, which in fact began its historical career in a phase of cultural evolution closely resembling that of the Pre-Islamic Arabs in the fourth-seventh centuries A.D. A century ago nothing was understood about the evolution of nomadism in Arabia; today we know that Pre-Islamic poetry reflects a stage of nomadic culture more than two thousands years later than the donkey nomadism of the ·Hebrew Patriarchs.

Wellhausen was not at all interested in the archaeological discoveries of the nineteenth century and virtually never referred to any of them. In fact, in his famous *History of Israel*, published in 1894, he did not even mention such a phenomenal discovery as that of the Amarna tablets. To men like Gunkel such finds proved decisively that Canaan already possessed an advanced civilization and maintained close relations with surrounding countries during the century before the time of Moses—who was, incidentally, quite correctly dated by Wellhausen to the thirteenth century B.C.

Against Wellhausen, Gunkel saw that the narratives of Genesis were a prose form of earlier poetic traditions, often going back to a high antiquity. These traditions were sometimes preserved in verse, but they usually appear in secondary prose form, though traces of the original verse composition may often be recognized by archaic language and poetic style. Gunkel was well aware of the great antiquity of the sagas of Genesis. He failed, however, to recognize that much "saga" is orally transmitted history, just as much "history" is a more sophisticated form of saga. It is hard to distinguish between saga and dramatic historical presentation. Besides, we now know that the traditions of Genesis had been handed down with extraordinary fidelity for many centuries before they were put into prose, usually in abbreviated form, about the tenth century B.C.

While Gunkel objected strenuously to Wellhausen's

view that most of the material preserved in Genesis is very late, he fully recognized the correctness of Wellhausen's sequence of documentary sources: J, E, P. He was, however, mistaken in following Wellhausen's dating of P as later than D, being misled by Wellhausen's own hyper-rigidity in dealing with legal material without adequate training in the history and development of law. Today we may confidently say that Gunkel was right in recognizing collectors instead of authors in the oldest sources. On the other hand, he was probably wrong in considering J and E as schools rather than as the work of single compilers or editors.

Martin Noth and the present writer have independently argued that J and E are so closely related that E can be considered only as a secondary recension of J. Moreover, as already recognized by Gunkel, it may also be shown that the narratives of P are in large part—though by no means entirely—later forms of JE.

Turning to the present state of our knowledge about the period described in Genesis, we may say that archaeological discoveries and improved interpretations of both unwritten and written materials recovered by excavators, have revolutionized our point of view completely. Wellhausen proves to have been wrong almost throughout, whereas Gunkel was right much of the time. In cases where Gunkel was mistaken, the state of our knowledge in 1901 was far too sketchy for positive conclusions. Now we have a multitude of archaeological discoveries from Palestine itself, from Syria, Mesopotamia, Egypt, and Asia Minor, all throwing light on the history of the early and middle centuries of the second millennium. Even when we do not have reference to persons and events in the narratives of the

Patriarchs, we almost invariably do have information about the life, culture, names of persons and places, laws, and customs of the time. These memories, though insufficient for political history, are of the greatest historical value in other respects, and they are directly illuminated by archaeological finds of all possible types. Without going into detail, we must emphasize the revolutionary significance of such cuneiform discoveries as the following: the Old Assyrian tablets from Cappadocia, the slightly later Mari tablets, the legal documents of the early second millennium from Babylonia, the Nuzi tablets (fifteenth century), the Amarna tablets (fourteenth century), the Hittite and Canaanite tablets (fifteenth-thirteenth centuries), etc. Since these documents run into the hundreds of thousands, and all belong to the period reflected by the Patriarchal narratives or not long afterwards, they are extraordinarily important for our understanding of Genesis. Note also that we have not yet mentioned the valuable background material from Egypt, such as the biography of Sinuhe, Semitic name lists, royal inscriptions, etc.

Thanks to these finds of written documents, supplemented by field-work, it is now possible to say with confidence that the stories of the Patriarchs contain a much higher proportion of matter bearing directly on history than they do of material obviously legendary or even mythological in origin—though the latter is also valuable for the light it sheds on the higher culture, religion, and literature of the Hebrews. For instance, we can now explain the occupational background of the early Patriarchs in a way totally impossible until a few years ago. Abraham turns out to have been a caravan leader, and the very name "Hebrew" refers

to donkey caravaneering. Donkey caravans are described in considerable detail, often with exact enumer-
ation of donkeys (which may run up to 3,000), in texts
ranging from about 2300 B.C. down to about 1700 B.C.
Camels may already have been domesticated in parts
of Arabia, but there is not a single reference to their
use in any document before the twelfth century B.C.
It has long been understood that the Hebrews were
stateless semi-nomads of chiefly Semitic stock; it had
not been recognized before 1961 that they must have
had some dominant occupation which would provide
them with a livelihood as well as a reason for their
wanderings between Babylonia and Egypt. The data
in Genesis make it possible for us to describe their occupational status in considerable detail, and we can
follow their wanderings from Ur in southern Babylonia
on to Harran in northwestern Mesopotamia. Then
we see the Patriarchs moving back and forth between
trading stations and caravan centers in Syria, Palestine,
and northern Egypt. The parallels between the life
of Genesis and the activities mentioned in contemporary
extra-biblical sources are very far-reaching indeed.

We have no more space to discuss these matters in
detail. So far as the evidence then indicated, Gunkel
saw truly; his mistakes were inevitable two-thirds of
a century ago, and do not detract from his epochal
place in the history of biblical scholarship.

I have checked the translation made by W. H. Carruth, and find it nearly always correct. Only one slip
was really bad; on page 29 he misread the German
erworben, "acquired," as *ermordet,* "murdered," but
this has been corrected in the reprinted text below.

In general it is a pity that Carruth chose the render-
ing "legends" for German *Sagen,* since German *Sage*

in its usual modern sense was taken over from Norse *saga*, which refers to a prose or more rarely a poetic narrative of historical origin or coloring. If we remember that Gunkel did not attempt to prejudge the historicity of a given narrative by calling it *Sage*—regardless of what "legend" may seem to mean in the context—we should not be misled.

W. F. ALBRIGHT

Baltimore, April 1964

The Legends of Genesis.

I.

THE SIGNIFICANCE AND SCOPE OF THE LEGENDS.

I.

THE SIGNIFICANCE AND SCOPE OF THE LEGENDS.

A RE the narratives of Genesis history or legend? For the modern historian this is no longer an open question; nevertheless it is important to get a clear notion of the bases of this modern position.

The writing of history is not an innate endowment of the human mind; it arose in the course of human history and at a definite stage of development. Uncivilised races do not write history; they are incapable of reproducing their experiences objectively, and have no interest in leaving to posterity an authentic account of the events of their times. Experiences fade before they are fairly cold, and fact and fancy mingle; only in poetical form, in song and saga, are unlettered tribes able to report historical occurrences. Only at a certain stage of civilisation has objectivity so grown and the interest in transmitting national experiences to posterity so increased that the writing of history becomes possible. Such history has for its subjects great

public events, the deeds of popular leaders and
kings, and especially wars.   Accordingly some sort
of political organisation is an antecedent presump-
tion to the writing of history.

Only in a later, in the main a much later, time is
the art of writing history, learned through the practice of writing national histories, applied to other
spheres of human life, whence we have memoirs
and the histories of families.   But considerable sections of the people have never risen to the appreciation of history proper, and have remained in the
stage of the saga, or in what in modern times is
analogous to saga.

Thus we find among the civilised peoples of
antiquity two distinct kinds of historical records
side by side: history proper and popular tradition,
the latter treating in naïve poetical fashion partly
the same subjects as the former, and partly the
events of older, prehistoric times.   And it is not to
be forgotten that historical memories may be preserved even in such traditions, although clothed in
poetic garb.

Even so did history originate in Israel.   In the
period from which the Book of Genesis is transmitted to us the art of history had been long established and highly developed according to ancient
standards, having for themes, here as everywhere, the
deeds of kings and especially wars.   A monument
of this history is found in the narratives of the
Second Book of Samuel.

But in a people with such a highly developed
poetical faculty as Israel there must have been a
place for saga too.   The senseless confusion of
"legend" with "lying" has caused good people to

hesitate to concede that there are legends in the Old Testament. But legends are not lies; on the contrary, they are a particular form of poetry. Why should not the lofty spirit of Old Testament religion, which employed so many varieties of poetry, indulge in this form also? For religion everywhere, the Israelite religion included, has especially cherished poetry and poetic narrative, since poetic narrative is much better qualified than prose to be the medium of religious thought. Genesis is a more intensely religious book than the Book of Kings.

There is no denying that there are legends in the Old Testament; consider for instance the stories of Samson and of Jonah. Accordingly it is not a matter of belief or skepticism, but merely a matter of obtaining better knowledge, to examine whether the narratives of Genesis are history or legend.

The objection is raised that Jesus and the Apostles clearly considered these accounts to be fact and not poetry. Suppose they did; the men of the New Testament are not presumed to have been exceptional men in such matters, but shared the point of view of their time. Hence we are not warranted in looking to the New Testament for a solution of questions in the literary history of the Old Testament.

CRITERIA FOR LEGEND AND HISTORY.

Now, since legend and history are very different in both origin and nature, there are many criteria by which they may be distinguished. One of the chief points of difference is that legend is originally oral tradition, while history is usually found in written form; this is inherent in the nature of the two species, legend being the tradition of those who are not in the habit of writing, while history, which is a sort of scientific activity, presupposes practice in writing. At the same time the writing down of an historical tradition serves to fix it, whereas oral tradition cannot remain uncorrupted for any length of time and is therefore inadequate to be the vehicle of history.

Now it is evident that Genesis contains the final sublimation into writing of a body of oral traditions. The tales of the patriarchs do not have the air of having been written down by the patriarchs themselves; on the contrary many passages reveal clearly the great interval of time that lies between the period of the patriarchs and that of the narrators. We read frequently the expression "even to this day," as in Genesis xix. 38; the kings of Edom are enumerated down to the time of David, xxxvi. 31 ff.; the sentence "in those days the Canaanites dwelt in the land" must have been written at a time when this race had long since passed away.

But the whole style of the narrative, as is to be shown hereafter, can be understood only on the supposition of its having been oral tradition; this state of the case can be realised especially through the many variants, to be treated in the following pages. But if the contents of Genesis is oral tradition, it is, as the preceding considerations show, legend also.

DIFFERENT SPHERES OF INTEREST.

Another distinguishing feature of legend and history is their different spheres of interest. History treats great public occurrences, while legend deals with things that interest the common people, with personal and private matters, and is fond of presenting even political affairs and personages so that they will attract popular attention. History would be expected to tell how and for what reasons David succeeded in delivering Israel from the Philistines; legend prefers to tell how the boy David once slew a Philistine giant.

How does the material of Genesis stand in the light of this distinction? With the exception of a single chapter (Chapter xiv), it contains no accounts of great political events, but treats rather the history of a family. We hear a quantity of details, which certainly have for the greater part no value for political history, whether they are attested or not: that Abraham was pious and magnanimous, and that he once put away his concubine to please his wife; that Jacob deceived his brother; that Rachel and Leah were jealous,—"unimportant anecdotes of country life, stories of springs, of watering-troughs, and such as are told in the bed-chamber," attractive enough to read, yet everything but historical occurrences. Such minor incidents aroused no public interest when they took place; the historian does not report them, but popular tradition and legend delight in such details.

EYE-WITNESS AND REPORTER.

In the case of every event that purports to be a credible historical memorandum, it must be possible to explain the connexion between the eye-witness of the event reported and the one who reports it. This is quite different in the case of legend, which depends for its material partly upon tradition and

partly upon imagination. We need only apply this
test to the first narratives of Genesis in order to
recognise their character straightway. No man was
present at the creation of the universe; no human
tradition extends back to the period of the origin of
our race, of the first peoples and the primitive lan-
guages.

In former times, before the deciphering of
hieroglyphs and cuneiform writing, it was possible
for Israelitic tradition to be regarded as so old that
it did not seem absurd to look to it for such reminiscences of prehistoric ages; but now when creation
has widened so mightily in our view, when we see
that the People of Israel is one of the youngest in
the group to which it belongs, there is an end of all
such conjectures. Between the origin of the primitive races of southwestern Asia and the appearance
of the People of Israel upon the stage of life had
rolled unnumbered millenniums; hence there is no
room for serious discussion over historical traditions
said to be possessed by Israel regarding those
primitive times.

The accounts of the patriarchs also give rise to
the most serious doubts. According to the tradition the period of the patriarchs is followed by the
four hundred years during which Israel lived in
Egypt. Nothing is reported from this latter period;
historical recollection seems to have been utterly
blotted out. And yet we have an abundance of
unimportant details regarding the period of the
patriarchs. How is it conceivable that a people
should preserve a great quantity of the very minut-
est details from the history of its primitive ancestors
and at the same time forget its own national history

for a long period following? It is not possible for oral tradition to preserve an authentic record of such details so vividly and for so long a time. And then, consider these narratives in detail. The question how the reporter could know of the things which he relates cannot be raised in most cases without exciting laughter. How does the reporter of the Deluge pretend to know the depth of the water? Are we to suppose that Noah took soundings? How is anyone supposed to know what God said or thought alone or in the councils of Heaven? (Cp. Genesis i. 2, 18, vi. 3-6 ff., xi. 6 ff.)

THE CRITERION OF INCREDIBILITY.

The clearest criterion of legend is that it frequently reports things which are quite incredible. This poetry has another sort of probability from that which obtains in prosaic life, and ancient Israel considered many things to be possible which to us seem impossible. Thus many things are reported in Genesis which go directly against our better knowledge: we know that there are too many species of animals for all to have been assembled in any ark; that Ararat is not the highest mountain on earth; that the "firmament of heaven," of which Genesis i. 6 ff. speaks, is not a reality, but an optical illusion; that the stars cannot have come into existence after plants, as Genesis ii. 10-14 reports; that the rivers of the earth do not come chiefly from four principal streams, as Genesis ii. thinks, that the Tigris and the Euphrates have not a common source, that the Dead Sea had been in existence long before human beings came to live in Palestine, instead of originating in historical times, and so on.

Of the many etymologies in Genesis the majority
are to be rejected according to the investigations of
modern philology. The theory on which the
legends of the patriarchs are based, that the nations
of the earth originated from the expansion of a
single family, in each case from a single ancestor,
is quite infantile.[1] Any other conclusion is impossible from the point of view of our modern historical
science, which is not a figment of imagination but
is based upon the observation of facts. And however cautious the modern historian may be in declaring anything impossible, he may declare with all
confidence that animals—serpents and she-asses, for
instance—do not speak and never have spoken, that
there is no tree whose fruit confers immortality or
knowledge, that angels and men do not have carnal
connexion, and that a world-conquering army cannot be defeated—as Genesis xiv. declares—with
three hundred and eighteen men.

WANING ANTHROPOMORPHISM.

The narratives of Genesis being mostly of a religious nature are constantly speaking of God. Now
the manner in which narratives speak of God is one
of the surest means of determining whether they are
historical or poetic. Here too the historian cannot
avoid having a universal point of view. We believe
that God works in the universe in the silent and
secret background of all things; sometimes his
influence seems almost tangible, as in the case of
exceptionally great and impressive events and per-
sonalities; we divine his control in the marvellous

---

[1] Compare my Commentary on Genesis, pp. 78 ff.

interdependence of things; but nowhere does he
appear as an operative factor beside others, but
always as the last and ultimate cause of everything.
Very different is the point of view of many of the
narratives in Genesis. We find God walking about
in the Garden of Eden; with his own hands he fash-
ions man and closes the door of the ark; he even
breathes his own breath into man's nostrils, and
makes unsuccessful experiments with animals; he
scents the sacrifice of Noah; he appears to Abraham
and Lot in the guise of a wayfarer, or, as an angel,
calls directly out of Heaven. Once, indeed, God
appears to Abraham in his proper form, having the
appearance of a burning torch and of a smoking bak-
ing-pot (the Revised Version in English has here
"furnace"). The speeches of God in Genesis are
remarkable for the fact that his words are not heard
in the obscure moments of intensest human excite-
ment, in the state of ecstasy, as was the case with
the prophets when they heard the voice of God, but
that God speaks in all respects as does one man to
another. We are able to comprehend this as the
naïve conception of the men of old, but we cannot
regard belief in the literal truth of such accounts as
an essential of religious conviction.

And these arguments are immensely strengthened
when we compare the narratives which on inner evidence we regard as poetry with the specimens which
we know of strict Israelitish history. For these
violations of probability and even of possibility are
not found throughout the Old Testament, but only
in certain definite portions possessing a uniform
tone, whereas they are not to be found in other portions which for other reasons we regard as more

strictly historical. Consider especially the central portion of the Second Book of Samuel, the history of the rebellion of Absalom, the most exquisite piece of early historical writing in Israel. The world that is there portrayed is the world that we know. In this world iron does not float and serpents do not speak; no god or angel appears like a person among other persons, but everything happens as we are used to seeing things happen. In a word, the distinction between legend and history is not injected into the Old Testament, but is to be found by any attentive reader already present in the Old Testament.

Moreover, it should not be forgotten that many of the legends of the Old Testament are not only similar to those of other nations, but are actually related to them by origin and nature. Now we cannot regard the story of the Deluge in Genesis as history and that of the Babylonians as legend; in fact, the account of the Deluge in Genesis is a younger version of the Babylonian legend. Neither can we reject all other cosmogonies as fiction and defend that of Genesis as history; on the contrary the account of Genesis i., greatly as it differs in its religious spirit from other cosmogonies, is by its literary method closely related to them.

LEGEND IS POETRY.

But the important point is and will remain the poetic tone of the narratives. History, which claims to inform us of what has actually happened, is in its very nature prose, while legend is by nature poetry, its aim being to please, to elevate, to inspire and to move. He who wishes to do justice to such narratives must have some æsthetic faculty, to catch in the telling of a story what it is and what it purports to be. And in doing so he is not expressing a hostile or even skeptical judgment, but simply studying lovingly the nature of his material. Whoever possesses heart and feeling must perceive, for instance in the case of the sacrifice of Isaac, that the important matter is not to establish certain historical facts, but to impart to the hearer the heartrending grief of the father who is commanded to sacrifice his child with his own hand, and then his boundless gratitude and joy when God's mercy releases him from this grievous trial. And every one who perceives the peculiar poetic charm of these old legends must feel irritated by the barbarian—for there are pious barbarians—who thinks he is putting the true value upon these narratives only when he treats them as prose and history.

The conclusion, then, that one of these narratives is legend is by no means intended to detract from the value of the narrative; it only means that the one who pronounces it has perceived somewhat of the poetic beauty of the narrative and thinks that he has thus arrived at an understanding of the story. Only ignorance can regard such a conclusion as irreverent, for it is the judgment of reverence and love. These poetic narratives are the most beautiful possession which a people brings down through the course of its history, and the legends of Israel, especially those of Genesis, are perhaps the most beautiful and most profound ever known on earth.

A child, indeed, unable to distinguish between reality and poetry, loses something when it is told that its dearest stories are "not true." But the

modern theologian should be further developed.
The evangelical churches and their chosen repre-
sentatives would do well not to dispute the fact that
Genesis contains legends—as has been done too
frequently—but to recognise that the knowledge of
this fact is the indispensable condition to an historical understanding of Genesis. This knowledge
is already too widely diffused among those trained
in historical study ever again to be suppressed. It
will surely spread among the masses of our people,
for the process is irresistible. Shall not we Evan-
gelicals take care that it be presented to them in the
right spirit?

II.

THE VARIETIES OF LEGENDS IN GENESIS.

II.

THE VARIETIES OF LEGENDS IN GENESIS.

IN the great mass of our materials two groups are
distinctly recognisable:

1. The legends of the origin of the world and of
the progenitors of the human race, the stories down
to the tower of Babel, their locality being remote
and their sphere of interest the whole world;

2. The legends of the patriarchs of Israel: Abraham, Isaac and Jacob, and the latter's sons, the
locality and the sphere of interest being Canaan and
adjacent lands.

Even in their character the two groups are most
plainly distinguished: the narratives of the first
group speak of God in a way different from that of
the legends of the patriarchs. In the latter the
divinity appears always enveloped in mystery,
unrecognised or speaking out of Heaven, or perhaps only in a dream. In the earlier legends, on
the contrary, God walks intimately among men and
no one marvels at it: in the legend of Paradise men
dwell in God's house; it is assumed that he is in the
habit of visiting them every evening; he even closes
the ark for Noah, and appears to him in person,
attracted by his sacrifice. Furthermore, in the
legends of the patriarchs the real actors are always
men; if the divinity appears, it is regarded as an

exception. But in the primitive legends the divinity is the leading actor (as in the creation), or at least among those chiefly concerned (as in the story of Paradise, of the union of men and of angels, of the Deluge and the Tower of Babel). This distinction is, to be sure, only relative, for some of the legends of the patriarchs (notably those connected with Hebron and Penuel) represent the divinity as appearing in the same way. On the other hand, the story of Cain and Abel and that of the cursing of Canaan, in which human beings are the chief actors, are among the primitive legends. However, the distinction applies on the whole to the two groups. This prominence of the action of the divinity in the primitive legends indicates that these have a more decidedly "mythical" character: that they are faded myths.

SOME LEGENDS ARE FADED MYTHS.

"Myths"—let no one shrink from the word—are stories of the gods, in contradistinction to the legends in which the actors are men. Stories of the gods are in all nations the oldest narratives; the legend as a literary variety has its origin in myths. Accordingly, when we find that these primitive legends are akin to myths, we must infer that they have come down to us in comparatively ancient form. They come from a period of Israel's history when the childlike belief of the people had not yet fully arrived at the conception of a divinity whose operations are shrouded in mystery. On the other hand, these original myths have reached us in comparatively faded colors. This we can perceive in the narratives themselves, where we are able in some points to reconstruct an older form of the story than the one transmitted to us: notably Genesis vi. 1-4 is nothing but a torso.

We are led to similar conclusions when we compare the primitive legends with the allusions to the myths which we find in the poets and prophets of the Old Testament and the later apocalyptic writers;[1] as, for instance, the myths of Jahveh's combat with Rahab or Leviathan, of the fall of Helal, and so on. The same result very clearly follows a comparison of the primitive legends of Genesis with the myths of the Orient, especially of the biblical story of the creation and the Deluge with the Babylonian versions of the same subjects. The colossal outlines, the peculiarly brilliant colors which characterise these myths in the original form are lost in a measure in the biblical legends of the beginnings of things. The equivalence of the divine beings and the objects or realms of nature, the combat of the gods with one another, the birth of the gods, are some of the features which have disappeared in the version of Genesis.

MONOTHEISM HOSTILE TO MYTHS.

In all this we can see the essential character of the religion of Israel. The fundamental trait of the religion of Jahveh is unfavorable to myths. For this religion from its very beginning tends toward monotheism. But for a story of the gods at least two gods are essential. Therefore the Israel which we observe in the Old Testament could not tolerate genuine and unmodified myths, at least not in prose.

[1] Compare the material gathered in my work *Creation and Chaos*, 1895.

The poet was excused for occasional allusions to myths. Hence in poetry we find preserved traces of a point of view older than that of the tradition of Genesis, one frankly familiar with myths. But the primitive legends preserved to us are all dominated by this unspoken aversion to mythology.

The monotheism of Israel tolerates only those myths that represent God as acting alone, as in the story of the creation, and even then there is no real "story," where action and counter-action give rise to a new situation or action. Or at the most, the story deals with action between God and men, where, however, men are too weak in the true Israelitish conception to be worthy rivals of God, to produce in their clash with God a real epic action; as soon as God intervenes all is decided. If in such a case a "story" is to be told, men must perform their part first. This is the method of the legends of Paradise and of the Tower of Babel. With the story of the Deluge it is different, God taking part from the beginning; but as a result of this the continued interest of the hearer is not maintained. Furthermore, it should be noted that the legends preserved to us with mythical elements are much less numerous than the legends of the patriarchs in which this element is absent. This fact also may fairly be regarded as a result of the Israelitish aversion to mythology.

THE SIGNIFICANCE OF MYTHS.

It is not proposed to present here a theory of the origin and primitive significance of myths. Only a few observations may be permitted. A certain series of myths may be interpreted on the assumption that some natural phenomenon that is wont to occur frequently or regularly in the actual world has furnished the colors for the painting of one similar but gigantic phenomenon in primitive times. Thus the creation of the world is painted as Spring on a grand scale, and the overflows of the rivers of Mesopotamia gave rise to the story of the Deluge.

Many myths attempt to answer questions, being intended to give instruction. This is the case with the primitive legends of Genesis: the story of creation raises the question, Whence come heaven and earth? and at the same time, Why is the Sabbath sacred? The story of Paradise treats the question, Whence are man's reason and his mortality? and along with this, Whence are man's body and mind? Whence his language? Whence the love of the sexes? Whence does it come that woman brings forth with so much pain, that man must till the stubborn field, that the serpent goes upon its belly, and so on? The legend of Babel asks the question, Whence is the variety of nations in language and location? The answers to these questions constitute the real content of the respective legends. In the case of the legend of the Deluge this is different, but there is an ætiological, or explanatory feature at the close: Why is there never such a flood again? And what is the meaning of the rainbow?

All these questions interest not Israel alone, but the whole world. We know that ancient Israel in general was not inclined to philosophic speculation, but that it always took most interest in immediate and Israelitish affairs. But here is a place in which the ancient race is able to treat universal human problems, the profoundest questions of mankind.

This they have done in unique fashion in the stories
of the creation and of Eden: these are the beginnings of theology and of philosophy.   It is no wonder that especial emphasis has been laid upon these
features, and that every generation, since Genesis
has been known, has read into it its own deepest
thoughts.

THE LEGENDS OF THE PARTIARCHS.

The primitive legends are followed in Genesis by
the legends of the patriarchs.   The distinctive
feature of these legends is that they tell of the progenitors of races, especially of Israel.   At the foundation of these legends lies the theory that all
races, Israel included, have come in each case from
the family of a single ancestor, which gradually
expanded.   This theory is not supported by
observed facts, for no human eye observes the origin
of races; on the contrary, it is the remnant of a
primitive poetic conception of tribal life.

In earliest times the individual man counts for
little.   There is much more interest in the destinies
of the race: the tribe, the nation, are regarded as
real entities much more than at the present day.
Thus it comes that the destinies of the race are
regarded as being the destinies of a person: the race
sighs, triumphs, is dejected, rebels, dies, comes to
life again, etc.   Thus too the relations of races are
regarded as the relations of individuals: two races
it is said, are brothers, i. e., are closely related and
equal; if one of them is regarded as richer, stronger,
or nobler, it is said to be the firstborn brother,
or it comes of a better mother, while the other
is younger, or comes of a concubine.   Israel being

divided into twelve tribes, we are told that the
tribal ancestor of Israel had twelve sons. Some of
these tribes having a closer union with one another,
they are said to come from one mother. The relation of mother and son exists between Hagar and
Ishmael; the more distant relation of uncle and
nephew between Abraham and Lot.

Originally these persons were the tribes themselves. This method of expression is still entirely
current later in the pathetic poetry of the prophets:
Edom builds his nest on high, Moab dies to the
sound of trumpets, Asshur falls upon Israel like a
lion upon his prey, Jerusalem and Samaria are two
unchaste sisters, Edom has treated his brother
Israel with enmity, etc. Such personifications must
have been very familiar to the earliest ages. But
as the world became more prosaic and these expressions were no longer understood in the simple narrative, the question was asked, who these persons,
Jacob, Judah, Simeon, really were, and the answer
given that they were the patriarchs and the later
races and tribes their sons; an answer which seems
to be a matter of course, since it was customary to
refer to the individual Israelites and Ammonites as
"Sons of Israel" and "Sons of Ammon."

PATRIARCHS REPRESENT TRIBES.

We are not putting a new meaning into the
legends which treat of such race-individuals, when
we regard their heroes, Ishmael, Jacob, Esau, and
others, as tribes and try to interpret the stories
about them as tribal events; we are simply getting
at their meaning as it was understood in primitive
times in Israel.

On the other hand, we must go about this attempt
with caution, for we must reckon with the possibility that some of these figures do not originally
represent tribes, but only came to be regarded as
patriarchs in a later time, and further, after the figures of the patriarchs had once become established
as the heroes of epic legends, that legends of other
sorts and wanting the basis of tribal history became
attached to these. We may certainly regard as
personifications of tribes those figures whose names
are known to us in othe᾿ connexions as names of
tribes; such are, notably: Ishmael, Ammon, Moab,
the twelve tribes and their divisions. Sometimes it
is perfectly evident from the narratives themselves
that we have to do with tribes, as in the case of
Cain and Abel, Jacob and Esau, Ham and Japhet.
Accordingly, many of the narratives treating such
ancestors are originally the experiences of races or
tribes.

Once in ancient times, so we may assume, there
were conflicts over wells between the citizens of
Gerar and the neighboring Bedouins, ending in a
compromise at Beersheba. The legend depicts these
affairs as a war and a treaty between Abimelech,
king of Gerar, and the patriarchs called in the
legend Abraham or Isaac. (xxi, 22 ff., 26.)

Dinah, the daughter of Jacob, is seduced by
Shechem, and in punishment Shechem is treacherously assaulted by Dinah's brothers; Jacob, however, abjures the brothers and curses them. The
history at the bottom of this is probably as follows:
Dinah, an Israelitish family, is overpowered by the
Canaanitish city of Shechem and then treacherously
avenged by Simeon and Levi, the most closely

related tribes, but the other tribes of Israel renounce them and allow the two tribes to be destroyed.

The legend of Tamar, also, depicts in part early relations in the tribe of Judah: Judah allied itself with Canaanites, in the legend Hirah of Adullam and Judah's wife, Bathshua; a number of Judæan-Canaanitish tribes (Er and Onan) perished early; finally two new tribes arose (Perez and Zerah). In the Esau-Jacob legend also there are quite evidently historical reminiscences: Esau and Jacob are brother tribes, Esau a tribe of hunters, Jacob a tribe of shepherds; Esau is the elder, but by sale or fraud he loses his birthright, that is, the older and better known tribe of Esau was compelled to give way to the later and originally weaker tribe of Jacob and has now the poorer land.

A similar rivalry is assumed by the legend between the Judæan tribes of Perez and Zerah and between Ephraim and Manasseh. Reuben, the first-born among the Israelitish tribes, loses his birthright on account of sin: the tribe of Reuben, which was the leading tribe in the earliest times, afterwards forfeited this position. Cain, the husbandman, slew his brother Abel, the herdsman, but was compelled to leave the land which they had before occupied in common. Shem, Japhet, and Canaan are originally brothers; but Japhet has now a much more extensive territory than the others, and Canaan is the servant of both.

We hear of many migrations. From the north Abraham migrates to Canaan, after him Rebeccah, to marry Isaac, and finally comes Jacob; the initial point of the migration is given as Ur-Kasdim and Haran the city of Nahor (xxiv. 10). In the legend

of Joseph there is described a migration of Israelitish tribes to Egypt; the account of the trip of
Abraham to Egypt has a similar basis.

Now it is in the nature of legend that we do not
catch sight of these old occurrences clearly by its
means, but only as through a mist. Legend has
woven a poetic veil about the historical memories
and hidden their outlines. In most cases the time
of the event is not to be derived from the legend
itself; often even the place is not to be distinguished, and sometimes not even the personality of
the actor. Who can tell what race it was that came
to Canaan from Aram-Naharajim? Where the real
home of Jacob and Esau was, of Cain and Abel, of
Shem and Japhet, the legend has forgotten. What
tribes parted at Bethel, in case there is any historical basis to the legend of the separation of Lot and
Abraham? And so, although the things of the past
are hidden rather than revealed in these legends,
he would be a barbarian who would despise them on
this account, for often they are more valuable than
would be prosaic reports of actual occurrences.
For instance, if we had good historical data regarding Ishmael we should not value them highly, for
this "wild ass" rendered little service to mankind;
but as it is, touched by the hand of poetry, he is
immortal.

In these legends the clearest matter is the character of races: here is Esau, the huntsman of the
steppes, living with little reflexion from hand to
mouth, forgetful, magnanimous, brave, and hairy as
a goat; and there is Jacob the herdsman, a smooth
man, more cunning and accustomed to look into the
future. His uncle Laban is the type of the

Aramæan, avaricious and deceitful, but to outward appearances an excellent and upright man, never at loss for an excuse. A more noble figure is Abraham, hospitable, peaceful, a model of piety.

Moreover it is clear to us in many cases in what spirit the incidents are regarded: we perceive most easily how the legend despises the unchastity of Canaan, how it mocks at Esau and Laban, how it rejoices that Lot, with all his avarice, obtained after all the worse land, etc.

ANTIQUITY OF THE LEGENDS.

These legends have not hitherto received full justice, even when it has been recognised that they are legends. Even the most superficial reader can distinguish for himself the chief original sources in Genesis from which the present redaction was constructed, now commonly called the writings of the Elohist, of the Jahvist, and of the Priestly Code. Since the sources of the Elohist and the Jahvist were written down in the ninth or eight century B. C., some commentators have been disposed to think that the legends themselves originated in the main in the age of the Israelitish kingdom and furnished therefore no revelations of primitive history. But in reality these legends are much older. The tribal and race names which they preserve are almost all forgotten in other records: we know nothing of Shem, Ham, and Japhet, of Abel and Cain, of Esau and Jacob, nothing of Hagar and scarcely anything of Ishmael, from the historical records of Israel. Hence we must conclude that these races all belong to prehistoric times. This is particularly evident in the case of Jacob and Esau, who were, to be sure, identified later with Israel and Edom. But this very lapping of names, as well as many features of the legend which are not applicable to Israel and Edom, as, for instance, the treaties between the city of Gerar and the sons of Abraham (or Isaac) concerning the possession of certain wells, especially that of Beersheba, show us that the old narrative originally had in mind entirely different races; in the legend Jacob is not disposed to war; in history Israel conquered Edom in war; in the legend Esau is stupid, in history he is famous for his wisdom.

Another proof of the age of these tribal legends may be found in the history of the legend in Israel. The legends in the Book of Judges have ceased to speak of tribes as persons (excepting Judges i.), but they tell of heroes, of individual leaders of the tribes. The latest story that preserves the old style and to which an historical date can be assigned is the legend of the capture of Shechem, the Dinah legend of Genesis. Sometime in the earlier portion of the period of Judges, then, this naïve style of narrative disappeared so far as we can ascertain; from that time on such narratives are merely transmitted, but no longer constructed new.

CLASSIFICATION OF LEGENDS.

We call these legends "historical" when they reflect historical occurrences, "ethnographic" when they contain chiefly descriptions of race and tribal relations. Thus we characterise the legend of the treaty of Beersheba and the various legends of migrations as "historical," but those of Jacob and Esau as "ethnographic."

ÆTIOLOGICAL LEGENDS.

Alongside these narratives of Genesis are also "ætiological" legends, that is, those that are written for a purpose, or to explain something. There is no end of the questions which interest a primitive people. The instinct for asking questions is innate in man: he wants to know of the origin of things. The child looks into the world with wide eyes and asks, Why? The answer which the child gives itself and with which it is for the time satisfied, is perhaps very childish, and hence incorrect, and yet, if it is a bright child the answer is interesting and touching even for the grown man. In the same way a primitive people asks similar questions and answers them as best it can. These questions are usually the same that we ourselves are asking and trying to answer in our scientific researches. Hence what we find in these legends are the beginnings of human science; only humble beginnings, of course, and yet venerable to us because they are beginnings, and at the same time peculiarly attractive and touching, for in these answers ancient Israel has uttered its most intimate feelings, clothing them in a bright garb of poetry. Some of these questions are the following:

ETHNOLOGICAL LEGENDS.

There is a desire to know the reasons for the relations of tribes. Why is Canaan the servant of his brethren? Why has Japhet such an extended territory? Why do the children of Lot dwell in the inhospitable East? How does it come that Reuben has lost his birthright? Why must Cain wander

about a restless fugitive? Why is sevenfold venge-
ance proclaimed against the slayer of Cain? Why
is Gilead the border between Israel and the Ara-
mæans? Why does Beersheba belong to us and not
to the people of Gerar? Why is Shechem in possession of Joseph? Why have we a right to the holy
places at Shechem and Machpelah? Why has
Ishmael become a Bedouin people with just this territory and this God? How does it come that the
Egyptian peasants have to bear the heavy tax of the
fifth, while the fields of the priests are exempt?
And with especial frequency the question was asked,
How does Israel come to have this glorious land of
Canaan?

The legends tell in many variations how it came
about that the patriarchs received this particular
land: God gave it to Abraham because of his
obedience; when on the occasion of the separation
at Bethel Lot chose the East, the West fell to
Abraham; Jacob obtained the blessing of the better
country from Isaac by a deception; God promised
it to Jacob at Bethel, and so on.

Such ethnological legends, which tell a fictitious
story in order to explain tribal relations, are of
course very difficult to distinguish from historical
legends which contain the remnant of a tradition of
some actual event. Very commonly ethnological
and ethnographic features are combined in the same
legend: the relations underlying the story are historical, but the way in which they are explained is
poetic.

The usual nature of the answer given to these
questions by our legends is that the present relations are due to some transaction of the patriarchs:

the tribal ancestor bought the holy place, and
accordingly it belongs to us, his heirs; the ancestors
of Israel and Aram established Gilead as their
mutual boundary; Cain's ancestor was condemned
to perpetual wandering by the word of God, and so
on. A favorite way is to find the explanation in a
miraculous utterance of God or some of the patriarchs, and the legend has to tell how this miraculous utterance came to be made in olden times.
And this sort of explanation was regarded as completely satisfactory, so that there came to be later
a distinct literary variety of "charm" or "'blessing." [1]

Childish as these explanations now seem to us,
and impossible as it was for the men of old to find
out the true reasons of such things, yet we must not
overlook the profundity of many of these poetic
legends: they are all based on the assumption that
the tribal and national relations of that day were
not due to chance, but that they were all the results
of events of the primitive world, that they were in a
way "predestined." In these legends we have the
first rudiments of a philosophy of history.

ETYMOLOGICAL LEGENDS.

Along with the above we find etymological
legends or features of legends, as it were, beginnings of the science of language. Ancient Israel
spent much thought upon the origin and the real
meaning of the names of races, mountains, wells,
sanctuaries, and cities. To them names were not
so unimportant as to us, for they were convinced
that names were somehow closely related to the

---

[1] Cp. Genesis xlix.

things. It was quite impossible in many cases for
the ancient people to give the correct explanation,
for names were, with Israel as with other nations,
among the most ancient possessions of the people,
coming down from extinct races or from far away
stages of the national language.   Many of our current names such as Rhine, Moselle, Neckar, Harz,
Berlin, London, Thames, Seine, etc., are equally
unintelligible to those not trained in philology.   It
is probable that the very fact of the oddity and
unintelligibility of these names attracted the attention of the ancient race.   Early Israel as a matter
of course explains such names without any scientific
spirit and wholly on the basis of the language as it
stood.   It identifies the old name with a modern
one which sounds more or less like it, and proceeds
to tell a little story explaining why this particular
word was uttered under these circumstances and was
adopted as the name.   We too have our popular
etymologies.   How many there are who believe
that the noble river which runs down between New
Hampshire and Vermont and across Massachusetts
and Connecticut is so named because it "connects"
the first two and "cuts" the latter two states!
Manhattan Island, it is said, was named from the
exclamation of a savage who was struck by the size
of a Dutch hat worn by an early burgher, "Man hat
on!"   Many are the stories told to explain why a
famous London highway is called "Rotten Row"
(*Route en roi*).

The Lombards, we are told by another legend,
were originally called Winili. But on an occasion
the women of the tribe put on beards as a disguise,
and Wodan looking out of his window in the morn-

ing exclaimed, "What are those 'long beards' (Lang-obarden)?" (Grimm, *German Legends*, No. 390.)

The famous Thuringian castle, the Wartburg, is said to have derived its name from the fact that the landgrave, having strayed thither during a hunt, exclaimed, *"Wart, Berg, du sollst mir eine Burg werden"* (Wait, mountain, thou shalt become my fortress).

Similar legends are numerous in Genesis and in later works. The city of Babel is named from the fact that God there confused human tongues (*balal*, xi. 9); Jacob is interpreted as "heelholder" because at birth he held his brother, whom he robbed of the birthright, by the heel (xxv. 26); Zoar means "trifle," because Lot said appealingly, "It is only a trifle' (xix. 20, 22); Beersheba is "the well of seven," because Abraham there gave Abimelech seven lambs (xxi. 28 ff.); Isaac (*Jishak*) is said to have his name from the fact that his mother laughed (*sahak*) when his birth was foretold to her (xviii. 12), and so forth.

In order to realise the utter naïveté of most of these interpretations, consider that the Hebrew legend calmly explains the Babylonian name Babel from the Hebrew vocabulary, and that the writers are often satisfied with merely approximate similar-ities of sounds: for instance Cain (more exactly *Kajin*) from *kaniti*, "I have acquired." (iv. 1), Reuben from *rah beonji*, "he hath regarded my misery" (xxix. 32), etc. Every student of Hebrew knows that these are not satisfactory etymologies. Investigators have not always fully perceived the naive character of this theory of etymology, but have allowed themselves to be misled into patching up some very unsatisfactory etymologies with modern appliances. In one case many theologians even are wont to declare one of these explanations, a very ingenious one indeed (Jahveh = "I am that I am," Ex. iii. 14) as an established etymology. But etymologies are not acquired by revelation. The etymological legends are especially valuable to us because they are especially clear illustrations of the ætiological variety of legend.

CEREMONIAL LEGENDS.

More important than these etymological legends are those whose purpose is to explain the regulations of religious ceremonials. Such ceremonial regulations play a great part in the life of primitive races, but many of these customs had become in part or altogether unintelligible to the one who observed them in the earliest times of which we have authentic record. For customs are far more persistent than opinions, and religious customs are particularly conservative. And even we, whose religious service has undergone a vigorous purging in the Reformation and again at the hands of rationalism, see and hear in our churches many things which we understand only in part or not at all.

Ancient Israel reflected deeply upon the origin of these religious practices. And if the grown people became too blunted by custom to be able to perceive the strange and unintelligible features of the custom, they were roused from their indifference by the questions of the children. When the children see their father perform all sorts of curious customs during the Feast of the Passover, they will ask— thus it is expressly told, Ex. xii. 26; xiii. 14—What

does this mean? and then the story of the Passover
is to be told them. A similar direction is given
with relation to the twelve stones in the Jordan
(Josh. iv. 6), which the father is to explain to the
children as memorials of the passage of the Jordan.
In these examples, then, we see clearly how such a
legend is the answer to a question. Similarly,
questions are asked with regard to the origin of
circumcision, and of the Sabbath. Why do we not
eat the muscle of the thigh? Why do they anoint
the holy stone of Bethel and deliver the tithes
there? Why do we not sacrifice a child at Jeruel as
Jahveh commands, but in its stead a ram (Gen.
xxii.)? Why do our people "limp," that is, perform a certain dance, at the festival in Penuel
(xxxii. 32)?

No Israelite could have given the real reason for
all these things, for they were too old. But to
relieve this embarrassment myth and legend step
in. They tell a story and explain the sacred custom: long ago an event occurred from which this
ceremony very naturally sprang, and we perform the
ceremony representing the event in commemoration
of it. But this story that explains the custom is
always laid in primitive times. Thus the ancient
race gives the entirely correct impression that the
customs of their religious service originated in the
immemorial past: the trees of Shechem and Hebron
are older than Abraham! We perform the rite of
circumcision in memory of Moses, whose firstborn
was circumcised as a redemption for Moses whose
blood God demanded (Ex. iv. 24 ff.). We rest on
the seventh day because God at the creation of the
world rested on the seventh day (a myth, because

God himself is the actor in it). The muscle of the thigh is sacred to us because God struck Jacob on this muscle while wrestling with him at Penuel (xxxii. 33). The stone at Bethel was first anointed by Jacob because it was his pillow in the night when God appeared to him (xxviii. 11 ff.). At Jeruel—this is the name of the scene of the sacrifice of Isaac, xxii. 1-19 (cf. the *Commentary*, p. 218 ff.) —God at first demanded of Abraham his child, but afterward accepted a ram. We "limp" at Penuel in imitation of Jacob, who limped there when his hip was lamed in the wrestling with God (xxxii. 32). And so on.

In all this matter we are constantly hearing of certain definite places, such as Bethel, Penuel, Shechem, Beersheba, Lacha-roi, Jeruel, etc., and of the trees, wells, and stone monuments at these places. These are the primitive sanctuaries of the tribes and families of Israel. Primitive times felt that there was some immediate manifestation of the nature of the divinity in these monuments, but a later time, which no longer regarded the connexion as so clear and so self-evident, raised the question, Why is this particular place and this sacred memorial so especially sacred? The regular answer to this question was, Because in this place the divinity appeared to our ancestor. In commemoration of this theophany we worship God in this place. Now in the history of religion it is of great significance that the ceremonial legend comes from a time when religious feeling no longer perceived as self-evident the divinity of the locality and the natural monument and had forgotten the significance of the sacred ceremony. Accordingly the legend has to supply

an explanation of how it came about that the God
and the tribal ancestor met in this particular place.

Abraham happened to be sitting under the tree in
the noonday heat just as the men appeared to him,
and for this reason the tree is sacred (xix. 1 ff.).
The well in the desert, Lacha-roi, became the sanctuary of Ishmael because his mother in her flight
into the desert met at this well the God who comforted her (xvi. 7 ff.). Jacob happened to be pass-
ing the night in a certain place and resting his head
upon a stone when he saw the heavenly ladder;
therefore this stone is our sanctuary (xxviii. 10 ff).
Moses chanced to come with his flocks to the holy
mountain and the thornbush (Ex. iii. 1 ff.). Probably every one of the greater sanctuaries of Israel
had some similar legend of its origin.

We can easily imagine that any such legend of a
sanctuary was originally told on the occasion of the
festival concerned and on the original spot, just as the
Feast of the Passover and the legend of the exodus,
the feast of Purim and the legend of Esther, the Babylonian Easter festival and the Babylonian hymn of
the creation, belong together, and as with us Christ-
mas and Easter are not to be thought of without
their stories. These ceremonial legends are so
valuable to us because we discover from them what
were the sacred places and customs of Israel and at
the same time they give us a very vivid realisation
of ancient religious feeling: they are our chief
sources of information regarding the oldest religion
of Israel. Genesis is full of them, and but few are
found in the later books. Almost everywhere in
Genesis where a certain place is named, and at
least wherever God appears at a definite place, it is

based on such a legend.   In these legends we have
the beginning of the history of religion.

GEOLOGICAL AND OTHER LEGENDS.

Aside from the foregoing we may distinguish a
number of other sorts of legends, of which at least
the geological deserves mention.   Such geological
legends undertake to explain the origin of a
locality.   Whence comes the Dead Sea with its
dreadful desert?   The region was cursed by God on
account of the terrible sin of its inhabitants.
Whence comes the pillar of salt yonder with its
resemblance to a woman?   That is a woman, Lot's
wife, turned into a pillar of salt in punishment for
attempting to spy out the mystery of God (xix. 26).
But whence does it come that the bit of territory
about Zoar is an exception to the general desolation?   Because Jahveh spared it as a refuge for Lot
(xix. 17-22).

All these ætiological legends, then, are remote
from the standards of the modern sciences to which
they correspond; we regard them with the emotion
with which a man looks back upon his childhood.
But even for our science they have a great value, for
they furnish us in their descriptions or implications
of definite conditions the most important material
for the knowledge of the ancient world.

MIXED LEGENDS.

Very frequently various types of legend are combined in one.   The flight of Hagar (xvi.) is to be
called ethnographic because it depicts the life of
Ishmael;   ethnologic, because it undertakes to
explain these conditions; in one feature it is allied

to the ceremonial legends, its explanation of the
sacredness of Lacha-roi; furthermore it has etymological elements in its interpetation of the names
Lacha-roi and Ishmael.—The legend of Paradise
treats all at once a number of questions.—The
legend of Bethel explains at once the worship at
Bethel and the name of the place.—The legends of
Beersheba (xxi., xxii. ff., xxvi.) contain remnants
of history, telling of a tribal treaty established
there, and at the same time certain religious
features, as the explanation of the sanctity of the
place, and finally some etymological elements.—The
legend of Penuel explains the sanctity of the place,
the ceremony of limping, and the names Penuel and
Israel. And so on. Etymological elements, it may
be noted, never appear alone in Genesis, but always
in connexion with other features.

ORIGIN OF THE LEGENDS.

In many cases the origin of the legends will have
been revealed with what has already been considered.
Thus, in most etymological legends it can be shown
quite clearly that those features in the legend which
explain the name were invented for this very purpose. The incident of Abraham's giving Abimelech
seven (sheba) lambs at Beersheba (xxi., 28 ff.) was
surely invented to explain this name; also the laugh-
ing (sahak) of Isaac's mother (xviii. 12-15), etc.
The narrative of Judah, Er, Onan (xxxviii.) and the
others is plainly nothing but a history of the Israelite families, just as the legend of Dinah (xxxiv.) is
merely a reflexion of the attack upon Shechem.
But, on the other hand, the investigator is to be
warned not to be too quick to jump at the con-

clusion that he always has the origin of the legend
in this oldest interpretation attainable by us.   On
the contrary, we have to reckon with the possibility
that the features of the story which are intelligible
to us were injected into it later, and that the legend
itself is older than any meaning we can see in it.

Finally, there are legends which cannot be classi-
fied under any of the heads given above.   Of such
are large portions of the legend of Joseph;   also the
chief feature of the story of Jacob and Laban;   the
deceits and tricks cannot be understood from the
standpoint of either history or ætiology.

The preceding classification of legends is based of
course upon the chief or dominant features.   Along
with these go the purely ornamental or æsthetic
features, twining about the others like vines over
their trellises.   The art of these legends is revealed
especially in this portrayal of the subject matter
given.

III.

THE LITERARY FORM OF THE LEGENDS.

III.

THE LITERARY FORM OF THE LEGENDS.

THE beauty of the legends of Genesis has always been a source of delight to readers of refined taste and it is not mere chance that painters have been so fond of choosing the subjects of their works from Genesis. Scholars have more rarely expressed appreciation of the beauty of these narratives, often perhaps for personal reasons, and perhaps often because the æsthetic point of view seemed to them incompatible with the dignity of science. However, we do not share this prejudice, but, on the contrary, are of the opinion that one who ignores the artistic form of these legends not only deprives himself of a great pleasure, but is unable properly to satisfy the scientific demands of the understanding of Genesis. Nay, more: it is no insignificant question for science to answer, in what the peculiar beauty of the legends consists,—a problem whose solution requires a thorough investigation of the contents and the religion of Genesis.

GENESIS IS PROSE.

The first question is, whether the form of the diction is prose or poetry. Aside from Genesis xlix. which is a poem and not a narrative, and on that

ground alone is out of place in Genesis, all that the
book contains is prose in form.   Detailed investigations of the nature of this prose have not been
carried on.   Meanwhile, at least this may be said,
that this prose is not the common colloquial language of every-day life, but is more artistic in its
composition and has some sort of rhythmical construction.   Hebrew prosody is still a sealed book
to us, but in reading Genesis aloud one feels an
agreeable harmony of rhythmically balanced mem-
bers.   The translator of Genesis is constrained to
imitate this balancing of sentences.

Since the legends were already very old when
they were written down, as will be shown hereafter, it is a matter of course that the language of
Genesis is somewhat archaic;   this too must be
reproduced in the translation.   In certain passages,
the climaxes of the stories, the language rises into
poetry, as is the case with the German *Märchen*
where the spells and charms are in poetic form.   In
the case of some of the legends we know variants
both Biblical and extra-Biblical, notably of the
stories of creation, of the Garden of Eden and of
the Flood, which are in strictly metrical form.
Inasmuch as these poetical variants are known to be
older than the prose versions transmitted in
Genesis, we are warranted in the conjecture that
the poetic form of these legends is older than any
prose form whatever.   The older and strictly
rhythmical form, which we must suppose to have
been sung, would differ from the later prose form,
which was recited, as does the ancient German epic
from the later *Volksbuch* (book of popular legends),
or as do the Arthurian poems of Christian of Troyes

from the prose versions of Mallory's *Morte d'Arthur*
or the Welsh Mabinogion.

GENESIS A FOLK-BOOK.

A second question is, whether these poetic versions are popular traditions or the productions of
individual poets. Modern investigators have
answered the general principle of the question to
the effect that Genesis is popular oral tradition
written down. We are able to explain clearly how
such popular traditions originate. Of course, in
the ultimate beginning it was always an individual
who improvised or devised this or that poem. But
it is characteristic of such popular traditions that
we are never able to observe them in the germ, any
more than we can in the case of language, but that
they appear, wherever we hear of them, as primitive possessions inherited from the patriarchs.
Between the poet who first conceived them and the
time when they were fixed for transmission to posterity a long period elapsed, and in this period the
legends were repeated from generation to generation and passed through many hands. Yet however
faithfully such legends are transmitted, they are
inevitably altered in the course of the centuries.
And thus they finally become the common product
of the people. This transformation of the legends
was unconscious, at least in its earlier stages. Only
in the more recent modifications is it reasonable to
assume the operation of conscious art.

Both narrators and auditors regarded the legends
as "true" stories. That this is true of the legends
of the Old Testament is shown in the historical
books of the Bible, where the narrators proceed by

almost imperceptible degrees from legends to genuine historical narratives. It follows also from the
legends themselves, which go about in all serious-
ness to account for actual conditions: because the
woman was made from man's rib, therefore he longs
for union with her; here we see that this story was
no mere poetical figure to the one who told it, but
an event that had actually happened. And furthermore, it is to be expected from the nature of the
case; legends come from ages and stages of civilisation which have not yet acquired the intellectual
power to distinguish between poetry and reality.
It is therefore no slight error when modern investigators declare the legend of Paradise to be an
allegory which was never intended to represent
actual occurrences.

Moreover, for the very reason that the legend is
the product of the whole people, it is the expression of the people's mind. And this is a point of
greatest importance for our interpretation of the
legends of Genesis. We are warranted in regarding the judgments and sentiments presented in Genesis as the common possession of large numbers of
people.

THE CONTENTS OF GENESIS IN PRIMITIVE FORM.

Accordingly, we should attempt in considering
Genesis to realise first of all the form of its contents
when they existed as oral tradition. This point of
view has been ignored altogether too much hitherto,
and investigators have instead treated the legendary
books too much as "books." If we desire to understand the legends better we must recall to view the
situations in which the legends were recited. We

hear of such situations Ex. xii. 26 f., xiii. 14 f.,
Joshua iv. 6: when the children ask about the reason
of the sacred ceremony then the father answers
them by telling the story. Similarly we can imagine
how the story of Sodom was told with the Dead Sea
in view, and the legend of Bethel on the summit of
Bethel. But the common situation which we have
to suppose is this: In the leisure of a winter evening the family sits about the hearth; the grown
people, but more especially the children, listen
intently to the beautiful old stories of the dawn of
the world, which they have heard so often yet never
tire of hearing repeated.

Many of the legends, as will be shown later, have
such a marked artistic style that they can scarcely
be regarded in this form as products of the collec-
tive people. On the contrary, we must assume that
there was in Israel, as well as among the Arabs, a
class of professional story-tellers. These popular
story-tellers, familiar with old songs and legends,
wandered about the country, and were probably to
be found regularly at the popular festivals.

We have already seen (page 38) that the transmitted prose narrative was perhaps preceded by a
narrative in regular rhythmical form and intended
for singing. In the case of these songs the circumstances of their presentation may have been different. From the precedent of the Babylonian poem
of the creation, which in its form is an Easter hymn
in praise of Marduk, we may infer that the legends
regarding forms of worship go back to hymns for
the sanctuary which were perhaps sung by the priest
at the sacred festivals and on the sacred ground (p.
33). But however this may be, the legends regard-

ing sanctuaries as we have them now had certainly
ceased to be sung, and, as their peculiarly colorless
attitude shows, were not connected with the sacred
place in this form, but belong already to popular
tradition.

THE REAL UNIT IN GENESIS.

A new and fundamental question is: What unit is
really the constituent unit in Genesis, the one which
we should first apply ourselves to? For there are a
number of different units in Genesis. The most
comprehensive unit is the whole Pentateuch, then
Genesis, and then the single collections of legends
that preceded it; then the individual legends of which
the book was composed. Among these a distinction has to be made between the independent individual legends, such, for example, as those of the
flight of Hagar and the sacrifice of Isaac, and on the
other hand certain groups of several legends con-
stituting legend-cycles, such as the cycle which
treats the destinies of Abraham and Lot down to
the birth of their sons, or the one comprising
Jacob's experiences with Esau and with Laban, or
the one of which Joseph is the hero. All of these
various units must be considered. But the first
question is, Which of these units is most important
for our purposes, that is, which of them was the
original unit in oral tradition?

This is a question that arises in many similar
cases: Which is the elemental unit: the song-book,
the individual group of songs in it, or the individual
song? Is it the gospel, the address, or the individual utterance that is reported of Jesus? The

whole apocalypse, the separate apocalyptic documentary sources, or the individual vision? For the
proper understanding of Genesis, also, it is of critical
importance that this question be clearly met and
correctly answered. Hitherto investigators have
seemed to regard it as a matter of course that the
original sources were the constituent units, though
the true view has not been without witnesses.[1]

Popular legends in their very nature exist in the
form of individual legends; not until later do compilers put several such legends together, or poets
construct of them greater and artistic compositions.
Thus it is also with the Hebrew popular legends.
The legends of Genesis even in their present form
give clear evidence of this. Every single legend
that is preserved in an early form is a complete
whole by itself; it begins with a distinct introduction and ends with a very recognisable close. Compare certain specific cases: Abraham wishes to sue
for a wife for his son; being too old himself he
sends out his oldest servant—thus the story opens.
Then we are told how the old servant finds the right
maiden and brings her home. Meantime the aged
master has died. The young master receives the
bride, and "he was comforted for the death of his
father." Everyone can see that the story ends here.

Abraham is directed by God to sacrifice his son;
this is the exposition (from xxii. on), which makes
an entirely new start. Then we are told how Abra-

---

[1] Reuss, AT III., p. 73: "Originally the legends of the
patriarchs arose individually without connexion and independently of one another."—Wellhausen, Composition 2, p. 9:
"Tradition in the popular mouth knows only individual
legends."

ham was resolved upon the deed and very nearly accomplished it, but at the last moment the sacrifice was prevented by God himself: Isaac is preserved to Abraham. "Then they returned together to Beer-sheba." We see that the narrative always opens in such a way that one recognises that something new is about to begin; and it closes at the point where the complication that has arisen is happily resolved: no one can ask, What followed?

Similarly, the unity of the separate legends is shown in the fact that they are in each case filled with a single harmonious sentiment. Thus, in the story of the sacrifice of Isaac, emotion is predominant; in that of Jacob's deception of Isaac, humor; in the story of Sodom, moral earnestness; in the story of Babel, the fear of Almighty God.

Many stories are entirely spoiled by following them up immediately with new ones which drive the reader suddenly from one mood to another. Every skilful story-teller, on the contrary, makes a pause after telling one such story, giving the imagination time to recover, allowing the hearer to reflect in quiet on what he has heard while the chords that have been struck are permitted to die away. Any one, for instance, who has followed the story of Isaac sympathetically, feels at the close the need of repose in which to recover from the emotion aroused. Those stories especially which aim to give a reason for some present condition (Cp. pp. 17, and 25-36) require a pause at the close so that the hearer may compare the prophecy and its present fulfilment; as evidence of this consider the close of the story of Eden, of the Flood, or of the drunkenness of Noah.

LEGEND CYCLES.

In later times there were formed of these individual legends greater units, called legend cycles, in which the separate legends are more or less artistically combined. But even here it is not at all difficult in most cases to extricate the original constituent elements from one another. Thus the legend cycle which treats Abraham and Lot separates clearly into the following stories: (1) The migration of Abraham and Lot to Canaan; (2) their separation at Bethel; (3) the theophany at Hebron; (4) the destruction of Sodom; (5) the birth of Ammon and Moab; (6) the birth of Isaac. The legend cycle of Jacob-Esau-Laban divised clearly into the legends of Jacob and Esau, of Jacob and Laban, the legends of the origin of the twelve tribes, with various legends interspersed of the origin of ritual observances. In the stories connected with Joseph, also, those of Joseph's intercourse with his brothers are clearly distinguished from those of Potiphar's wife, of Pharaoh's dreams, and those of the agricultural conditions of Egypt (Gen. xlvii. 13-26).

This leads to the practical conclusion for the exegete that each individual legend must be interpreted first of all from within. The more independent a story is, the more sure we may be that it is preserved in its original form. And the connexion between individual legends is of later origin in many cases, if it be not simply an hallucination of the exegete.

As an example of a primitive legend which is almost wholly without antecedent assumptions, take the story of Hagar's flight, Gen. xvi., for which we need to know only that there is a man named Abraham with a wife named Sarah; everything else is told by the legend itself. An example of a later narrative is that of the suit for the hand of Rebeccah (chap. xxiv.): this legend is based upon a whole series of individual elements which belong to other legends, as the kinship and migration of Abraham, the promise of Jahveh at the migration, the facts that Isaac was his only son and the son of his old age, and so forth. Hence it is the individual legend with which we shall have to deal first in this treatise.

LENGTH OF LEGENDS.

What are the limits of such a story? Many of the stories of Genesis extend over scarcely more than ten verses. This is the case with the stories of Noah's drunkenness, of the tower of Babel, of Abraham's journey to Egypt, of Hagar's flight or the exile of Ishmael, of the trial of Abraham, of Jacob at Bethel and at Penuel. After these very brief stories we can group a series of more detailed stories occupying about a chapter, such as the story of Paradise, of Cain's parricide, of the Flood, of the theophany at Hebron, of the betrothal of Rebeccah, of the fraud perpetrated upon Isaac by Jacob. Finally the legend cycles exceed this limit of space.

This matter of the compass of the legends constitutes a decided distinction between them and our modern productions. Even the most complex legend groups of Genesis, such as that of Joseph, are of very modest extent by modern standards, while the older legends are absolutely abrupt to modern taste. Now, of course, the brief compass of the old legends is at the same time an index of

their character. They deal with very simple occurrences which can be adequately described in a few
words. And this compass accords also with the
artistic ability of the narrator and the comprehension of the hearer. The earliest story-tellers were
not capable of constructing artistic works of any
considerable extent; neither could they expect their
hearers to follow them with undiminished interest
for days and even weeks continuously. On the contrary, primitive times were satisfied with quite brief
productions which required not much over half an
hour. Then when the narrative is finished the
imagination of the hearer is satisfied and his attention exhausted.

On the other hand, our narratives show us that
later times were no longer satisfied with the very
brief stories of primitive construction; a more fully
developed æsthetic faculty demands more scope for
its expression. Thus greater compositions arose.
This growth in the compass of legends was favored
by the circumstance of their being written down;
written productions are naturally more discursive
than oral ones, because the eye in reading can more
easily grasp larger conceptions than the ear in hearing. Accordingly, this too is a measure of the
relative age of legends, though a measure which
must be used with caution: the briefer a legend, the
greater the probability that we have it in its original form.

SIMPLICITY AND CLEARNESS OF PRIMITIVE LITERARY ART.

The brevity of the legends is, as we have seen, a
mark of the poverty of primitive literary art; but at

the same time this poverty has its peculiar advantages. The narrow limits within which the narrator moves compel him to concentrate his entire poetic power into the smallest compass; so that, while these creations are small, they are also condensed and effective. And the moderate grasp which these small works of art have to reckon upon in their hearers results also in making the narratives as clear and synoptic as possible.

To make this last fact more evident, consider in the first place the balance of parts. Not only the longer of these narratives, but especially the briefest also are outlined with extraordinary sharpness. Thus, the story of Noah's drunkenness is constructed as follows: Exposition, Noah's drunkenness. I. The occurrences: (1) Canaan's shamelessness; (2) the filial respect of Shem and Japhet; II. The judgments: (1) concerning Canaan; (2) concerning Shem and Japhet.—Or take the story of the Garden of Eden, chap. iii.: I. The sin: (1) the serpent tempts Eve; (2) the woman and the man sin; (3) as consequence, the loss of their innocence; II. The examination; III. The punishments: (1) the curse upon the serpent, (2) upon the woman, (3) upon the man; IV. Conclusion: the expulsion from the garden.

By means of such plain and beautiful analyses the narratives gain in clearness, that is, in the prerequisite of all æsthetic charm: the whole is analysed into divisions and subdivisions which are themselves easily grasped and the relation of which to one another is perfectly plain. And these outlines are never painfully forced, but seem to have come quite as a matter of course from the nature of the subject.

Consider, for instance, in the story of Eden, how perfectly the outline corresponds to the contents: in the fall the order is: Serpent, woman, man; the examination begins with the last result and reverses the process, the order here being: Man, woman, serpent; the punishment falls first upon the chief sinner, and accordingly the original order is here resumed: Serpent, woman, man. Hence the modern reader is advised to heed the systematic arrangement of parts, since the analysis will at the same time give him the course of the action.

Furthermore, the narrator of the legend, unlike the modern novelist, could not expect his hearers to be interested in many persons at once, but on the contrary, he always introduces to us a very small number. Of course the minimum is two, because it takes at least two to make a complication of interests: such are the cases of the separation of Abraham and Lot, of Esau's sale of his birthright, and of the story of Penuel; there are three personages in the story of the creation of the woman (God, the man and the woman), in the story of Cain's fratricide (God, Cain and Abel), in the story of Lot in the cave, and of the sacrifice of Isaac; there are four in the story of Eden, of Abraham's journey into Egypt, of Hagar's flight, of the deception practised upon Isaac by Jacob.

There are indeed narratives in which more personages take part, as in the case of the detailed story of the suit for the hand of Rebeccah, and especially in the stories of the twelve sons of Jacob. Yet even here the narrators have not been neglectful of clearness and distinctness. In very many cases where a number of persons appear, the many are treated as

one: they think and wish the same things and act
all alike: thus in the story of the Flood and of the
tower of Babel all mankind are treated as one person, so also with the brothers Shem and Japhet,
with the three men at Hebron and at Sodom
(according to the original version of the story),
Lot's son-in-law at Sodom, the courtiers of Pharaoh,
the citizens of Shechem (Gen. xxxiv. 24), the
brothers of Dinah (xxxiv. 25), the citizens of
Temnah (xxxviii. 24), and in many other cases.
This is in accord with the conditions of antiquity,
in which the individual was much less sharply distinguished from the mass of the people than in
modern times.   At the same time, however, this
condensation of several persons into one is due to
the inability of the narrator to catch and depict the
actual distinctions among individuals.

How limited in those days the capacity of even
an artistically developed narrator to depict character is shown in the conspicuous instance of the
story of Joseph: the narrative presents Joseph and
the eleven in conflict; among the others the story
distinguishes Joseph's full brother, Benjamin, the
youngest; of the remaining ten Reuben (Judah) is
recognised separately.   But this is the extent of the
narrator's power to characterise; the remaining nine
lack all individuality; they are simply "the
brothers."

Further simplicity is attained by means of the
arrangement of parts, which, as we have noted,
resolves the story into a number of little scenes.
And in these scenes it is rare that all the persons of
the story appear at once, but only a few, usually
only two, are shown us at once.   Compare the

scenes of the story of the suit for Rebeccah; the
first scene shows Abraham and his servant, the
second shows the servant alone on the journey and
at the well, the third the servant and the maiden,
the fourth the maiden and her family, the fifth, and
principal, scene shows the servant together with
the maiden in her home, the sixth the servant
returning home with the maiden, the last their
arrival at the tent of Isaac. Or, another instance,
the story of the exile of Ishmael (xxiv. 4 ff.) shows
in succession: Sarah hearing the daughter of
Ishmael, and persuading Abraham; Abraham
expelling Hagar; then Hagar alone in the wilderness with the child, and finally her rescue by the
angel. The story of Jacob's deception (xxvii.)
treats first of Isaac and Esau, then of Rebeccah and
Jacob, next of Jacob before Isaac, and of Esau
before Isaac, of Esau's hatred of Jacob, and finally
of Rebeccah's advice to Jacob.

The narrative takes especial pains to motivate this
succession of scenes; and yet it does not hesitate to
simply drop a personage on occasion, as in the case
of the serpent after the temptation, or of Rebeccah
after the death of Isaac. By means of this analysis
the narrative gains great clearness; the hearer is not
constrained to keep a confusing group of people in
view, but he sees them in succession; thus he has
time to inspect them at leisure and to familiarise
himself with them. Only once, at the climax of
the action, do all the persons appear together: thus
in the story of Eden, in that of Noah's drunkenness,
and in the story of Joseph at the close. But even
here the narrators considered grouping necessary.
They would not have been able to conduct a con-

versation between a number of persons at once.
Thus at the end of the story of Eden God does not
reprove all the participants in one common address;
but he turns first to the serpent, then to the woman,
then to the man. And elsewhere also it is the
nature of the style to divide up the conversation
into so many dialogues.

CHIEF AND SUBORDINATE PERSONAGES.

The survey of the various personages is further
facilitated by a very distinct separation of leading
and subordinate parts. The hearer does not have to
ask many questions to learn which of the personages should receive his especial attention; the narrator makes this very plain to him simply by speaking
most of the chief personage. Thus in most of the
legends of the patriarchs the patriarchs themselves
are as a matter of course the chief personages. In
the following cases the personages of their respective stories are arranged in the order in which they
interest the narrator: Cain, Abel; Abraham, Sarah,
Pharaoh (Genesis xii. 10-20); Abraham, Lot;
Hagar, Sarah, Abraham (chap. xvi.); the servant
and Rebeccah are the chief personages in chap.
xxiv., the others being all of second rank; in chap.
xxvii. the chief personages are Jacob and Esau,
while the parents are secondary; in the story of
Jacob and Laban these are the chief personages, the
women secondary. In this classification sympathy
and veneration are not to be confused with interest;
the artistic interest of the narrator is greater in
Cain than in Abel, in Hagar than in Sarah; in chap.
xxiv, the servant is the chief personage while Abraham has only a subordinate part.—In many cases it

is the destinies of a single leading personage that we pursue, noticeably in the case of the stories of Joseph.

DESCRIPTION OF CHARACTERS.

In attempting to discover the' method by which characters are depicted we are first struck by the brevity with which subordinate personages are treated. Modern literary creations have accustomed us to expect that every personage introduced be characterised if possible with at least a few touches as an independent individual. The method of the primitive saga-man is entirely different. The personages whom he considers altogether or temporarily subordinate receive little or no characterisation. In view of the primitive feeling on the subject it is a matter of course that not much attention was paid to slaves. The attendants of Esau (xxxii. ff.) or of Laban (xxxi. 23) are introduced merely to show their masters' importance, and have no further significance. The narrators did not even consider it necessary to mention the sin of the two chamberlains of Pharaoh (xli. 1), or the feelings of Dinah (xxxiv.), or those of Sarah on the journey to Egypt (xii. 10 ff.). Hirah, the friend of Judah (xxxviii. 1, 12, 20), is not characterised; the sin of Er (xxxvii. 7) is not specified; nothing is told of Shuah, the wife of Judah (xxxviii. 2-12), that is really characteristic; the same is true of Joseph's steward (xliii. 16), of Potiphar, and others.

And even the characterisation of the chief personages is remarkably brief according to our notions. Only a few traits are ascribed to them, often but one. Cain is jealous of his brother, Canaan is

shameless, Shem and Japhet respectful. In the
story of the separation of Lot and Abraham, the
former is greedy, the latter conciliatory. In the
story of Hebron, Abraham is hospitable, and in the
migration he is obedient to the will of God. In
the story of Penuel, Jacob is strong and brave, in
the affair with Esau he is crafty, in the story of
Joseph he is fond of the children of Rachel. In
the somewhat complex story of the Fall the serpent
is crafty and evil, the man and the woman are
guileless as children, the woman is fond of dainties
and gullible , the man follows his wife. Even in
the case of God each individual story as a rule
speaks of but one single quality: in most of the
legends he is the gracious helper, in others, as the
stories of Paradise and Babel, he is the lofty sovereign whose concern is to keep men within bounds.

We are struck by this paucity in the legends, since
we are familiar in modern compositions with portraits made up of many separate traits and painted
with artistic detail. The art of the primitive story-
tellers is very different. True, it is based upon the
actual conditions of primitive ages in one respect:
the men of antiquity were in general more simple
than the many-sided men of modern times. Yet it
would be an error to suppose that men in those
earlier days were as simple as they are represented
to be in the legends; compare in evidence of this
the character sketches of a somewhat maturer art in
the Second Book of Samuel. With this example in
mind we shall recognise also that there is some
other ground for the brevity of the legends of
Genesis than that abbreviation of the real which is
inevitable in every artistic reproduction of life.

POPULAR LEGENDS TREAT MEN AS TYPES.

It is, on the contrary, a peculiar popular conception of man that we meet in Genesis. This conception was unable to grasp and represent many sides of man, much less all; it could see but a little. But so much the more need had it to catch the essential traits of the individual, wherefore it constructed types. Thus in the story of the flight of Hagar, Hagar is the type of the slave (xvi.) who is too well treated, Sarah of the jealous wife, Abraham the type of the conciliatory husband. Rachel and Leah are types of the favorite and of the unloved wife; in the story of the migration of Abraham to Egypt, or the story of Joseph, Pharoah acts like the typical Oriental king in such cases; his courtiers are courtiers and nothing more; Abraham's servant, chap. xxiv., is an old and tried servant; Isaac, in the story of the deception, is a blind old man, and Rebeccah a cunning, partial mother; Abraham in his migration and in chap. xxii. is the type of the pious and obedient man. A number of figures are the types of the races which are said to be descended from them: the shameless Canaan, the generous but stupid Esau, the crafty Laban, the still more crafty Jacob (cp. p. 23).

Doubtless it is another sign of the lack of creative grasp when the legends thus present to our eyes species instead of individuals; but the narrators have made a virtue of necessity. Within the limited sphere assigned to them they give us extraordinary achievements. The types which they had the opportunity to observe they have depicted with a confidence and a clearness similar to those displayed in the national types preserved to us by the

Egyptian painters. And for this very reason many of the old legends still fascinate the modern reader, and even the unlearned reader; they often reproduce universally human conditions and relations which are intelligible without interpretation unto this day. To the special student, however, they yield much greater pleasure, for to him they furnish the most intimate revelations regarding primitive conditions and sentiments.

As a natural conclusion from this simplicity of the characters represented we recognise that the art of these popular legends was far from undertaking to show any development in the characters, such as improvement or degeneration. Not that primitive times ignored the possibilities of such changes; the denunciations of the prophets as well as historical evidence prove the contrary. But the art of the story-teller is far from equal to the task of depicting such an inward change. All that modern exegetes claim to have found in Genesis in this line is simply imported into the sources: Jacob's dishonest character did not change at all; and Joseph's brethren are not at all reformed in the course of the story, but simply punished.

While, therefore, the individual legends recognise in the main only one quality of the personages involved, the legend cycles are able to give more detailed descriptions, although after a peculiar manner. The characteristic instance is, of course, the portrayal of the figure of Joseph in the cycle of legends devoted to his history. Here each individual legend brings out one or two sides of his nature: one legend (xxxvii.) tells us that he was loved by his father and therefore hated by his

brethren, and that he had dreams; another (xxxix.)
tells us that everything throve under his hand, and
that he was fair and chaste; a third (xl.) that he
could interpret dreams; and a fourth (xli.) that he
was crafty; and so on. Combining all these individual traits we get finally a complete portrait.

Furthermore, the narrators are exceedingly grudg-
ing in the outward description of their personages:
they reveal nothing regarding hair, complexion,
eyes or garb. In all this they seem to take the
normal Hebrew type for granted. And wherever
they deviate from this rule in their description it is
done for specific reasons: Esau is red and hairy
(xxv. 25) clearly because he is a type of the
Edomite; Jóseph wears his long garment with
sleeves (xxxvii. 3) as a badge of the love of his
father; Leah had "tender eyes" and Rachel is beautiful of form (xxix. 17) to explain why Jacob rejects
Leah and loves Rachel.

Now if we ask what principle the story-teller follows when he does emphasise definite characteristics
of his personages, we discover that the characterisation is generally subordinated to the action. The
particular quality of the person is emphasised that
is necessary for the development of the action; all
others are ignored. The story of the deception
practised by Jacob tells how the latter, following
his mother's counsel, induces his father to bless him
instead of Esau: here Jacob is crafty, he practises
deception; Esau is stupid, he lets himself be
cheated; Isaac is easily deceived, is blind; Rebeccah is cunning, she gives the deceitful advice and
is partial to Jacob. This is further portrayed in a
more detailed narrative: Jacob is a shepherd who

dwells at home with his mother, Esau a hunter whose venison the father is fond of. The modern story-teller would add a quantity of further traits to give color and life to the figures, but the primitive story-teller rejected all such details. It is very easy to see what the æsthetic interest of the narrator was: he cared above all things for the action; the portrayal of figures was for him only a secondary matter.

METHODS OF THE NARRATORS.

What means do the narrators use for the representation of the character of their heroes? The modern artist is very apt to explain in extended descriptions the thoughts and feelings of his personages. When one turns from such a modern story-teller to the study of Genesis, one is astonished to find in it so few utterances regarding the inner life of the heroes. Only rarely are the thoughts of even a leading personage expressly told, as in the case of the woman when she was looking desirously at the tree of knowledge, or of Noah, when he sent forth the birds "to see whether the waters were dried up off the earth," or the thoughts of Lot's sons-in-law, who judged that their father-in-law was jesting; the thoughts of Isaac, who feared at Gerar that he might be robbed of his wife (xxvi. 7); or the cunning thoughts with which Jacob proposed to evade the revenge of his brother Esau (xxxii. 9), and so on. But how brief and unsatisfactory even this appears compared with the psychological descriptions of modern writers!

And even such examples as these are not the rule in the legends of Genesis. On the contrary, the narrator is usually content with a very brief hint, such as, "He grew wroth" (iv. 5; xxx. 2; xxxi. 36; xxxiv. 7; xxxix. 19; xl. 2), or, "He was afraid" (xxvi. 7; xxviii. 17; xxxii. 8), "He was comforted" (xxiv. 16), "He loved her" (xxiv. 67; xxix. 18; xxx. 3; xxxvii. 3), "She became jealous" (xxx. 1), "He was filled with fear" (xxvii. 33), "He eyed him with hatred" (xxvii. 41; xxxvii. 4), and elsewhere. But even these brief hints are far from frequent; on the contrary, we find very often not the slightest expression regarding the thoughts and feelings of the person concerned, and this in situations where we cannot avoid a certain surprise at the absence of such expressions. The narrator tells us nothing of the reasons why God forbade man to partake of the fruit of the tree of knowledge, nor of the reasons of the serpent for wishing to seduce mankind. He says nothing of the feelings with which Abraham left his home, or Noah entered the ark. We do not learn that Noah was angry at Canaan's shamelessness, that Jacob was disappointed when Laban cheated him with Leah, that Hagar was glad when she received the promise that Ishmael should become a great nation; we are not even told that mothers rejoice when they hold their firstborn son in their arms. Particularly striking is the case of the story of the sacrifice of Isaac: what modern writer would fail under such circumstances to portray the spiritual state of Abraham when his religious devotion wins the hard victory over his parental love, and when his sadness is finally turned into rejoicing!

THOUGHT EXPRESSED BY ACTIONS.

Now what is the reason for this strange proceeding? We can find it in an instance like that of xix. 27 ff. In sight of the city of Sodom Abraham had heard certain remarkable utterances from the three men; they had said that they were going down to Sodom to examine into the guilt of the city. This strange remark he let run in his head; in the morning of the following day he arose and went to the same place to see whether anything had happened in Sodom during the night. And in fact, he sees in the valley below a smoke, whence he must infer that something has taken place; but this smoke hides the region, and he cannot make out what has happened. For the story-teller this little scene is plainly not of interest because of the thing that happens, but because of the thoughts which Abraham must have thought, and yet he does not tell us what these thoughts were. He merely reports to us the outward incidents, and we are obliged to supply the really important point ourselves. This story-teller, then, has an eye for the soul-life of his hero, but he cannot conceive these inward processes with sufficient clearness to express them in definite words.

This is a typical instance for Genesis. In very many situations where the modern writer would expect a psychological analysis, the primitive story-teller simply presents an action. The spiritual state of the man and woman in Paradise and after the Fall is not analysed, but a single objective touch is given by which we may recognise it. The narrator says nothing of the thoughts of Adam when

the woman handed him the forbidden fruit, but
merely, that he ate it; he does not discourse to us
on Abraham's hospitable disposition, but he tells us
how he entertained the three men.   He does not say
that Shem and Japhet felt chastely and respectfully,
but he has them act chastely and respectfully; not
that Joseph had compassion upon his brethren, but
that he turned away and wept (xlii. 24; xliii. 30); not
that Hagar, when mistreated by Sarah, felt offended
in the depths of her maternal pride, but that she ran
away from her mistress (xvi. 6); not that Laban was
dazzled by the gold of the stranger, but that he made
haste to invite him (xxiv. 30); not that obedience
to God triumphed in Abraham over parental love,
but that he arose straightway (xxii. 3); not that
Tamar remained faithful to her husband even beyond the grave, but that she took measures to rear
up children from his seed (xxxviii).

From all this we see on what the story-teller laid
the chief emphasis.   He does not share the modern
point of view that the most interesting and worthy
theme for art is the soul-life of man; his childlike
taste is fondest of the outward, objective facts.
And in this line his achievements are excellent.
He has an extraordinary faculty for selecting just
the action which is most characteristic for the state
of feeling of his hero.   How could filial piety be
better represented than in the story of Shem and
Japhet?   Or mother-love better than by the behavior
of Hagar?   She gave her son to drink—we are not
told that she herself drank.   How could hospitality
be better depicted than in the actions of Abraham
at Hebron?   And there is nothing less than genius
in the simple manner in which the innocence and

the consciousness of the first men is illustrated by their nakedness and their clothing.

These simple artists had not learned how to reflect; but they were masters of observation. It is chiefly this admirable art of indirectly depicting men through their actions which makes the legends so vivid. Little as these primitive men could talk about their soul-life, we gain the impression that they are letting us look into the very hearts of their heroes. These figures live before our eyes, and hence the modern reader, charmed by the luminous clearness of these old legends, is quite willing to forget their defects.

SOUL-LIFE NOT IGNORED.

But even when the story-teller said nothing of the soul-life of his heroes, his hearer did not entirely fail to catch an impression of it. We must recall at this point that we are dealing with orally recited stories. Between narrator and hearer there is another link than that of words; the tone of the voice talks, the expression of the face or the gestures of the narrator. Joy and grief, love, anger, jealousy, hatred, emotion, and all the other moods of his heroes, shared by the narrator, were thus imparted to his hearers without the utterance of a word.

Modern exegesis is called to the task of reading between the lines the spiritual life which the narrator did not expressly utter. This is not always such a simple matter. We have in some cases gotten out of touch with the emotions of older times and the expressions for them. Why, for instance, did Rebeccah veil herself when she caught sight of

Isaac? (xxiv. 25.)   Why did the daughters of Lot go
in unto him?   Why did Tamar desire offspring of
Judah? (xxxvii.)   What is the connexion of the
awakening modesty of the first men and their sin?
In such cases exegesis has often gone far astray by
taking modern motives and points of view for
granted.

A further medium of expression for the spiritual
life of the personages is articulate speech.   Words
are not, it is true, so vivid as actions, but to make
up for this they can the better reveal the inner life
of the personages.   The early story-tellers were
masters in the art of finding words that suit the
mood of the speakers: thus the malice of the cunning serpent is expressed in words, as well as the
guilelessness of the childlike woman, Sarah's jealousy of her slave as well as the conciliatoriness of
Abraham (xvi. 6), the righteous wrath of Abimelech
(xx. 9), the caution of the shrewd Jacob (xxxii. 9),
and the bitter lament of Esau (xxvii. 36) and of
Laban (xxxi. 43) when deceived by Jacob.   Notable
masterpieces of the portrayal of character in words
are the temptation of the first couple and the conversation between Abraham and Isaac on the way to
the mount of sacrifice.

LACONISM OF THE LEGEND WRITERS.

But even in this connexion we find many things
to surprise us.   First of all, that the personages of
Genesis often fail to speak where the modern writer
would surely have them do so, and where the very
nature of the case seems to require it.   We may
well imagine that Joseph complained aloud when

he was cast into the pit and carried away to Egypt (cp. also xlii. 21), that the murder of Abel was preceded by a dispute, that Hagar left Abraham's house weeping and complaining that Abraham had put her away (xxi. 14); but there is nothing of the kind. The first couple do not utter a word of reply when God pronounces his curse upon their future: they do not even indulge in self-accusations; not a word does Rebeccah say in chapter xxvi., nor Noah during the Deluge, nor Abraham in chapter xviii, when a son is promised him or when he is commanded to sacrifice Isaac; neither does Hagar when she sees her child dying, nor later when God heard the weeping of Ishmael. One who examined these references might easily conclude that the personages of Genesis were intended to be portrayed as taciturn and even secretive; he would find the only talkative individual to be—God.

But if we go more deeply into these legends, we perceive that this extraordinary laconism is part of the style of the narrator. The narrators subordinated everything to the action. They introduced only such speeches as really advanced the action. Hence especially they avoided giving utterance to the feelings of the merely passive personages. Whether Joseph complains or keeps silence, when his brethren sell him, makes no difference with his destiny. What words were spoken by Abraham and Noah when they received the commands of God makes no difference; suffice it, they obeyed. The destiny of the first family is fixed when God has cursed them; no self-reproaches will help the matter. Or, what do we care about the dispute that preceded the murder of Abel, since we know the reason which prompted Cain's deed! And it appears perfectly natural that men should make no reply to the promises of God, as is usually the case; for what can man add when God has spoken?

The other side of this strangely laconic method is that the remarks which the narrator does introduce are an essential part of the narrative. The conversation between the serpent and the woman is to show how it came about that the forbidden fruit was eaten. Cain pours forth his guilt-laden heart before God, and as a result modifies his sentence. Abraham begs his wife to declare herself his sister; and thus it comes about that she was taken into the harem of Pharaoh (xii. 11 ff.). Abraham gave Lot the choice of going to the east or to the west; hence Lot chose the plain of the Jordan. At Sarah's request Abraham takes Hagar as concubine and at her request he gives her up again. In these cases the words are not idle; on the contrary they are necessary to suggest an inner motive for the action to follow. Especially necessary are the words of cursing and of promise; they are the very climax of the story, up to which all the rest leads. This explains why God is so often represented as speaking in Genesis; for speech is really the chief medium through which God influences the action in these legends.

In some places the narrators have introduced monologues, the most unconcrete of all forms of speech, when the situation showed that there was no one present to whom the person could have spoken. This is quite commonly the case with God; for to whom should God reveal his most hidden decrees? But in a few cases we can infer (i. 26; ii. 6 f.) an elder form of the account, in which God addressed himself to his celestial associates.

But even in the laconic legends there are speeches which, while they are not exactly necessary, either characterise a person or attempt to give the opinion of the narrator, or which aim at some other point which the narrator wants to make. Many of the speeches in Genesis are exceedingly brief. Recall the lament of Hagar: "I am fleeing before the face of my mistress" (xvi. 8), or the words of the daughters of Lot (xix. 31), of Sarah (xxi. 10), of Abraham (xxi. 24), "I will swear," of Rebeccah (xxiv. 18 ff.), of Jacob (xxv. 33), "Swear to me this day," of Isaac (xxvi. 7), "She is my sister," of the shepherds of Gerar (xxvi. 20), "The water is ours," of Isaac's slaves (xxvi. 32), "We have found water," of Laban (xxix. 14), "Yea, thou art my flesh and blood," and so on. Of course, the speeches are not always so brief; they are especially apt to grow longer in the solemn and impressive formulæ of cursing and blessing. But in general we may see in brevity a characteristic mark of a certain type in Genesis.

Even such utterances do not always reveal the ultimate purpose of the actors, and reveal their spiritual life only in an indirect way. Hence the expressions are not always entirely clear for us, and require an especial gift for their interpretation. We are told that God forbade to man the fruit of the tree of life, but his reason for this is not given. What thought was in God's mind when threatening man with immediate death, whereas this result did not actually follow? So, too, we learn that the serpent desires to betray the woman, but not his reason. And even such psychological masterpieces as the story of the temptation are only indirect portrayals of soul-life.

NO NATURE-LOVE IN GENESIS.

Very many of the legends are no less laconic in their descriptions of incidental circumstances. In this respect also there is a great difference between the primitive literary art and that of modern story-tellers. Of course, the ancients have no touch of the intimate feeling for the landscape; there is no trace of nature-love in Genesis. The facts that the story of Eden is set among green trees, the story of Hagar in the barren desolation of the wilderness, the story of Joseph in the land of the Nile, affect the course of the story in certain respects, indeed, since the first pair clothe themselves with leaves and since the desert is a place where one can get lost, and where there is no water. But these facts in no wise affect the mood or sentiment of the action.

ECONOMY OF DETAILS.

But aside from this intimate feeling for the life of nature, which was foreign to the primitive man, how easy it would have been to give a description of Paradise! What modern poet would have missed the opportunity! But the early story-tellers were content to say that there were beautiful trees there, and the source of mighty rivers. It is a piece of the same method that the narrator does not tell us with what weapon Cain slew Abel; he tells us merely that Noah planted vines and then that he

drank of the wine, omitting the intervening steps
of picking and pressing the grapes; he no more tells
us how the contempt of Hagar was expressed (xvi.
4) than how Sarah took her revenge. We are wont
to admire the circumstantiality of the narratives,
and justly, but this by no means implies that the
legends abound in striking and highly concrete
touches; on the contrary, they present on the whole
not an abundance, but a paucity, of concrete elements. But the little that we have is so judiciously
selected that we are warranted in seeking for a purpose in almost every minute feature.

This economy of circumstantial details is the
more striking because alongside such lightly
sketched features, and especially in the more
detailed narratives, there are often very minute
descriptions. Thus, for instance, the meal that
Abraham serves to the three men is described in
detail, while the meal of Lot is but briefly
sketched. For the purpose of exegesis it is very
suggestive to keep this question constantly in mind,
to observe the brief and detailed treatments, and to
consider everywhere the interest of the narrator.
In general this will warrant the conclusion that the
narrator portrays the principal events concretely,
while merely hinting at or omitting those which
are incidental to the action: thus, for instance, in
the story of the sacrifice of Isaac the three days'
journey is covered at a bound, while the short passage to the place of sacrifice is described in all
detail. The narrator is quite arbitrary in the matter. Similarly the experiences of Abraham's servant
on the day when he sued for the hand of Rebeccah
are reported very minutely, while all the days con-

sumed in the journey to the city of Nahor are disposed of in a breath.

This emphasis laid upon the action is seen also in the manner of the conclusion of the narrative. The legends stop promptly when they have attained the desired object, not with a gradual cadence, but with a sudden jolt. This observation also is important for exegesis. The point just before the close is recognised as the climax by the narrator. Yet there are here two varieties of conclusion: the customary sort follows the climax with a short sentence (the type is the sacrifice of Isaac); the less common, and plainly more impressive, closes with a pathetic address (the curse of Noah is here the type).

UNITY AND COHERENCE OF PARTS.

From the above observations we conclude that in the primitive legends everything is subordinated to the action. In other literatures there are narratives in which the action is merely a garb or a thread, while the chief concern is the psychologic study, the brilliant conversation, or the idea; but not so with the primitive Hebrew legend. The primitive man demanded from his story-teller first of all action; he demands that something shall happen in the story to please his eye. But the first essential in such a story is to him its inner unity; the narrator must furnish him a connected series of events each necessarily dependent on the preceding.

One of the chief charms of the early legend is just this: to show how one thing resulted from another. The more plausible and necessary this connexion appears, the more attractive seems the whole story. A famine forces Abraham to go to Egypt; but he is

afraid of being killed there on account of his beautiful wife. *Therefore* he reports his wife to be his
sister. Deceived *by this* Pharaoh takes Sarah and
makes presents to Abraham. *Therefore* God pun-
ishes Pharaoh. *In consequence of this* Pharaoh
releases Sarah but permits Abraham to retain the
presents.—Sarah has no children, but desires them.
Therefore she gives her maid to Abraham as concubine. *Thus* Hagar conceives by Abraham.
Hence Hagar despises her mistress. *This* offends
the proud Sarah most deeply. *Therefore* she causes
Abraham to restore Hagar to her, and mistreats her.
As a result Hagar flees into the desert. *Here* God
has compassion on her and promises her a son.

Observe how in such cases each successive member is linked to the preceding one; how each preceding member appears as the natural cause or at
least the antecedent of the succeeding one. We are
in the habit, following a sort of tradition, of calling
this kind of narrative childish; but in so doing we
are only partially right.

These narratives, then, are exceedingly tense in
their connexion. The narrators do not like digres-
sions, but press with all their energy toward the
mark. Hence they avoid, if possible, the introduction of new features in a given story, but seek an
uninterrupted connexion. Rarely indeed are new
assumptions introduced, but good style demands the
announcement of all assumptions as near the beginning as possible. In pursuit of this method it is
considered permissible to skip over the necessary
consequences of what has been told, provided only
that those features stand forth which are essential to
the continuation of the action. There must be

nothing too much, and nothing too little.   The narrator does not spring aside; but the hearer also
must not be allowed to spring aside: the narrator
holds fast to him so that he can think only what the
narrator wants to have him think.

VARIATIONS ON A GIVEN THEME.

Many of the legends are fond of varying a given
motive.   Consider how the story of Eden makes
everything dependent on the nakedness and the
clothing of man, and how the relation of "field"
and "field-tiller" (this is the etymology of the
Hebrew word here used for "man") pervades this
whole legend; how the story of Joseph's sale into
Egypt treats the coat-sleeve (coat of many colors)
and the dreams; how the story of Jacob's last testament (xlvii. 29 ff.) constantly connects his actions
with his bed: in praying he bows at the head of the
bed, xlvii. 31; in blessing he rises up in bed,
xlviii. 2; in dying he stretches himself out upon his
bed, xlix. 33 (English version: "gathered up his
feet in his bed"), and so on.   In this the rule is,
quite in opposition to our sense of style, to repeat
the expression every time the thing is referred to,
so that one and the same word often runs through
the story like a red thread.   Undoubtedly this custom originated in the poverty of the language; but
the narrators of our legends follow it in order to
produce an impression of unity and simplicity.

Precisely because of this inward connexion in the
story it is possible in many places where our
received text shows gaps or distortions to recognise
the original form of the legend: the text-criticism
is in this point very much more positive than in the

case of the prophets, the laws and the songs, which lacked this connected condensation.

PLAUSIBILITY DEMANDED.

Furthermore, the course of the action must be probable, highly credible, even unavoidable. Nowhere must the hearer be able to make the objection that what is being told is inconsistent with what has preceded or with itself. Hagar, when elevated to too high station, could not fail to grow haughty; and Sarah could not help feeling offended. True, the probability aimed at by these old story-tellers was different from that of which we speak. Their understanding of nature was different from ours; for instance, they regarded it as entirely credible that all the kinds of animals could get into the ark; furthermore, the way in which they speak of God and his participation in the affairs of the world was naïver than is possible for us of modern times; they regarded it as quite plausible that the serpent should have spoken in primitive times; that Joseph, the grand vizier, should look after the sale of the corn in person.

Hence it would be quite unwarranted to speak of the "arbitrariness" and "childish recklessness" of the legends simply because the assumptions of the narrators are impossible to us in modern times. Only in a very few places can the eye of the modern reader, even though trained for criticism, detect improbabilities. In this line we may ask why Joseph, who was so much attached to his father, failed to communicate with him all the long years. Even after Hagar and her son were once rescued, were not the dangers of the desert sure to recur

every day? But the auditor of ancient times
doubtless did not ask such questions; he was more
willing to surrender to the narrator, and was more
easily charmed; he was also more credulous than we
are; compare for instance, xliii. 23.

SUSTAINED INTEREST.

On the other hand, in a well-told legend the incidents are not so simple that one can guess the whole
course of events from the first few words; if it were
so, the legend would lose its interest. No one
cares to hear of things that are self-evident. On
the contrary, our story-tellers are dealing with what
they regard as a complicated situation, whose final
outcome cannot be surveyed in advance by the
hearer. This leads him to listen the more intently.
Jacob wrestles with a supernatural being; which of
the two will conquer? Jacob and Laban are equally
gifted in cunning; which will succeed in deceiving
the other? The shrewd but unwarlike Jacob has to
meet the dull but physically superior Esau; how
will he manage him? Abraham has to go down
into Egypt, and how will he fare there? Thus all
these stories are more or less exciting. The childlike listener holds his breath, and rejoices when the
hero finally escapes all the threatening dangers.

The narrators are very fond of contrasts: the
child cast out into the desert becomes a mighty
people; a poor slave, languishing in prison,
becomes the ruler of Egypt with all her abundance.
They try if possible to focus these contrasts into a
single point: at the moment when Hagar is in utter
despair, God takes compassion on her; the very
instant when Abraham raises his arm to slay Isaac,

he is checked by God.   Lot lingers, and Jacob holds the divinity fast until the dawn is at hand: the next moment will surely bring the decision.

And where this intense interest is wholly lacking, where there is no complication of interests, there we have no real legend.   Thus the account of creation in Genesis i. is scarcely to be called a story; and yet, from v. 2 and 26, as well as from the poetic versions referred to on pp. 10-12 and 25-26, we can conjecture a form of the account in which more personages appear and in which the world is created after a conflict of God with Chaos.   In like manner, the accounts of Abraham's migration and of his league with Abimelech are not real legends, but only legendary traditions which have originated probably from the decay of earlier and fuller legends.

LEGENDS NOT PURE INVENTION.

As we have seen in the second division of this treatise, the legends are not free inventions of the imagination.   On the contrary, a legend adopts and works over certain data which come from reflexion, tradition or observation.   These fundamental data have been treated in the preceding pages; our present task is to consider the part taken by the imagination in the development of the legends.   With this subject we have reached the very heart of our investigations.

As has been shown above, many of the legends seem intended to answer definite questions.   That is, these legends are not the thoughtless play of an imagination acting without other purpose than the search for the beautiful, but they have a specific purpose, a point, which is to instruct. Accordingly, if these narratives are to attain their object they must make this point very clear. They do this in a decided way, so decidedly that even we late-born moderns can see the point clearly, and can infer from it the question answered. The sympathetic reader who has followed the unhappy-happy Hagar on her way through the desert will find no word in the whole story more touching that the one which puts an end to all her distress: God hears. But this word contains at the same time the point aimed at, for upon this the narrator wished to build the interpretation of the name Ishmael ("God hears").—Or what word in the legend of the sacrifice of Isaac stamps itself so deeply upon the memory as the affecting word with which Abraham from the depths of his breaking heart quiets the questioning of his unsuspecting child: God will provide! This word, which made God himself a reality, is so emphasised because it answers the question after the etymology of the place (Jeruel).

Other legends reflect historic events or situations, and in such cases it was the duty of the narrator to bring out these references clearly enough to satisfy his well-informed hearer. Thus in the legend of the flight of Hagar the actors are at first mere individuals whose destinies are interesting enough, to be sure, but at the climax, with the words of God regarding Ishmael the narrator shows that in Ishmael he is treating of a race and its destinies.

Hebrew taste is especially fond of playing about the names of leading heroes and places, even when no etymology is involved Many of the legends are quite filled with such references to names. Thus the legend of the Deluge plays with the name of Noah (cp. viii. 4, 9, 21), the story of the sacrifice of Isaac with Jeruel (xxii. 8, 12, 13), the story of the meeting of Jacob and Esau with Mahanaim and Penuel (cp. p. 321 in my *Commentary*), and so on.

Thus these legends are rich in points and allusions; they are so to speak transparent: even the one who reads them naïvely and simply as beautiful stories finds pleasure in them, but only the one who holds them up against the light of the primitive understanding can catch all their beautiful colors; to him they appear as small but flashing and brilliant works of art. The characteristic feature of the Hebrew popular legends as contrasted with other legends, if we understand the matter, consists in the flashing of these points.

The art of the story-tellers consists in avoiding every suspicion of deliberate purpose at the same time that they give great prominence to their point. With marvellous elegance, with fascinating grace, they manage to reach the goal they have set. They tell a little story so charmingly and with such fidelity to nature that we listen to them all unsuspecting; and all at once, before we expect it, they are at their goal. For instance, the story of Hagar's flight (xvi.) wishes to explain how Ishmael, although the child of our Abraham, was born in the wilderness; to this end it draws a picture of Abraham's household: it shows how, by an entirely credible series of events, Ishmael's mother while with child was brought to desperation and fled into the wilderness; thence it came that Ishmael is a child of the desert.

In many cases the task of the narrator was very

complex: he had to answer a whole series of different questions, or to assimilate a quantity of antecedent presumptions. Thus, one variant of the legend
of Babel asks the origin of the difference of lan-
guages and of the city of Babel, the other wants to
know the source of the distribution of races and
also of a certain ancient structure. Or again, the
story of Abraham at Hebron undertakes to tell not
only the origin of the worship at Hebron, but also
to explain the birth of Isaac and the choice of his
name. Here then the task was, to unite the differing elements into unity. And it is just here that
the story-tellers show their art. The prime motive
furnishes the leading thread of the story; the subordinate motives they spin into a single scene which
they introduce into the body of the story with easy
grace.

ETYMOLOGIES SUBORDINATE FEATURES.

The etymologies usually constitute such subordinate motives. Thus in the story of the worship at
Jeruel a scene is interjected which is to explain the
name of the place, "God sees"; but this little
scene, the dialogue between Abraham and Isaac,
xxii. 7 f., expresses so completely the tone and
sentiment of the whole story that we should not be
willing to dispense with it even if it had no particular point of its own. In other cases the artists
have joined together two leading motives; then
they invented a very simple and plausible transition from one to the other: thus the first part of the
legend of Hebron presents the establishment of
worship there under the guise of the story that

Abraham entertained the three divine visitors there;
the second portion, which is to account for the birth
of Isaac, simply proceeds with the given situation,
having the three guests enter into a conversation at
table and therein promise Isaac to Abraham.   It is
the most charming portion of the task of the inter-
preter of Genesis to search for these matters, and
not only, so far as this is possible, to discover what
is for us the oldest meaning of the legends, but also
to observe the refinements of artistic composition
in the stories.

SUMMARY.

We have to do, then, even in the oldest· legends
of Genesis, not with aimless, rude stories, tossed off
without reflexion, but on the contrary, there is
revealed in them a mature, perfected, and very
forcible art.   The narratives have a very decided
style.

Finally, attention should be called to the fact that
the narrators scarcely ever express a distinct opinion about persons or facts.   This constitutes a clear
distinction between them and the later legends and
histories worked over under the influence of the
prophets.   Of course, the narrators of the early
legends had their opinions; they are by no means
objective, but rather intensely subjective; and often
the real comprehension of the legend lies in our
obtaining an impression of this opinion of the narrator.   But they almost never gave expression to
this opinion: they were not able to reflect clearly
on psychological processes.   Wherever we do get
a more distinct view of such an opinion it is by

means of the speeches of the actors which throw some light on what has happened; consider particularly the utterances of Abraham and Abimelech, chapter xx., or the final scene of the story of Laban and Jacob, xxxi. 26 ff. At the same time this suppression of opinions shows most clearly that the narrators, especially the earlier ones, did not care to proclaim general truths.

It is true, there are at the basis of many of the legends and more or less distinctly recognisable, certain general truths, as, in the case of the story of the migration of Abraham, a thought of the value of faith, and in the story of Hebron, the thought of the reward of hospitality. But we must not imagine that these narratives aimed primarily at these truths; they do not aim to teach moral truths. With myths, as has been shown on pages 15-17, this is different, for they aim to answer questions of a general nature.

AN EARLY ISRAELITISH ROMANCE

Out of the type of legend which has been sketched in essentials in the preceding pages there was evolved, as we may discover even in Genesis itself, another type relatively much nearer to modern fiction. While the story of Hagar's flight is a classic instance of the former sort, the most conspicuous example of the second is the story of Joseph. It is necessary only to compare the two narratives in order to see the great differences in the two kinds: there, everything characteristically brief and condensed, here, just as characteristically, everything long spun out.

The first striking difference is the extent of the stories. Since the earlier form was in vogue we see that men have learned to construct more considerable works of art and are fond of doing so. The second is, that people are no longer satisfied to tell a single legend by itself, but have the gift of combining several legends into a whole. Thus it is in the story of Joseph, so also in the Jacob-Esau-Laban story and in the legends of Abraham and Lot.

Let us inquire how these combinations came about. In the first place, related legends attracted one another. For instance, it was to be expected that legends treating the same individual would constitute themselves into a small epic, as in the stories of Joseph and of Jacob; or the similar, and yet characteristically different, legends of Abraham at Hebron and Lot at Sodom have become united. Similarly in J, a story of the creation and a story of Paradise are interwoven; both of them treat the beginnings of the race. In P the primitive legends of the creation and of the deluge originally constituted a connected whole. In many cases that we can observe the nature of the union is identical: the more important legend is split in two and the less important one put into the gap. We call this device in composition, which is very common in the history of literature — instance *The Arabian Nights*, the *Decameron*, *Gil Blas*, and Hauff's *Tales*— "enframed stories." Thus, the story of Esau and Jacob is the frame for the story of Jacob and Laban; the experiences of Joseph in Egypt are fitted into the story of Joseph and his brethren; similarly the story of Abraham at Hebron is united with that of Lot at Sodom.

DEVICES FOR UNITING SEVERAL STORIES.

In order to judge of the artistic quality of these compositions we must first of all examine the joints or edges of the elder stories. Usually the narrators make the transition by means of very simple devices from one of the stories to the other. The transition par excellence is the journey. When the first portion of the Jacob-Esau legend is finished Jacob sets out for Aram; there he has his experiences with Laban, and then returns to Esau. In the story of Joseph the carrying off of Joseph to Egypt, and later the journey of his brethren thither, are the connecting links of the separate stories. Similarly in the story of Abraham and Lot, we are first told that the three men visited Abraham and went afterwards to Sodom.

Now we must examine how these various journeys are motivated. The sale of Joseph into Egypt is the goal at which everything that precedes has aimed. The journey of his brethren to Egypt is prompted by the same great famine which had already been the decisive factor in bringing Joseph to honor in Egypt. And the experiences of the brethren in Egypt are based upon Joseph's advancement. Thus we see that the story of Joseph is very cunningly blended into a whole.

There is less of unity in the story of Jacob; but even here there is a plausible motive why Jacob goes to Laban: he is fleeing from Esau. In other respects we find here the original legends side by side unblended. On the contrary, in the story of Abraham and Lot no reason is alleged why the three men go directly from Abraham to Sodom; that is to say, there is here no attempt at an inner harmonising of the different legends, but the narrator has exerted himself all the more to devise artificial links of connexion; this is why he tells that Abraham accompanied the men to the gates of Sodom, and even returned to the same place on the following morning. In this we receive most clearly the impression of conscious art, which is trying to make from originally disconnected elements a more plausible unity. In the Joseph legend we have an instance of a much more intimate blending of parts than the "frames" of these other stories, a whole series of different adventures harmonised and interwoven.

EPIC DISCURSIVENESS.

Another characteristic feature of the Joseph story is its discursiveness, which stands in notable contrast with the brevity of the older narratives. We find in it an abundance of long speeches, of soliloquies, of detailed descriptions of situations, of expositions of the thoughts of the personages. The narrator is fond of repeating in the form of a speech what he has already told. What are we to think of this "epic discursiveness"? Not as an especial characteristic of this particular narrative alone, for we find the same qualities, though less pronounced, in the stories of the wooing of Rebeccah, of Abraham at the court of Abimelech (Genesis xx.), in some features of the story of Jacob (notably the meeting of Jacob and Esau); and the stories of the sacrifice of Isaac and various features of the story of Abraham and Lot also furnish parallels.

Very evidently we have to do here with a distinct

art of story-telling, the development of a new taste.
This new art is not satisfied, like its predecessor,
with telling the legend in the briefest possible way
and with suppressing so far as possible all incidental
details; but it aims to make the legend richer and to
develop its beauties even when they are quite incidental. It endeavors to keep situations that are
felt to be attractive and interesting before the eye
of the hearers as long as possible. Thus, for
instance, the distress of Joseph's brethren as they
stand before their brother is portrayed at length;
there is evident intent to delay the narrative, so that
the hearer may have time to get the full flavor of
the charm of the situation. Thus Joseph is not permitted to discover himself at the very first meeting,
in order that this scene may be repeated; he is made
to demand that Benjamin be brought before him,
because the aged Jacob hesitates a long time to obey
this demand, and thus the action is retarded. Similarly in the story of the sacrifice of Isaac, the narrative is spun out just before the appearance of God
upon the scene, in order to postpone the catastrophe
and intensify the interest.

The means that is applied over and over again to
prolong the account is to report the same scene
twice, though of course with variations. Joseph
interprets dreams for Egyptian officials twice;
Joseph's brethren must meet him in Egypt twice;
twice he hides valuables in their grain sacks in
order to embarrass them (xlii. 25 ff., xliv. 2 ff.);
twice they bargain over Joseph's cup with the
steward and with Joseph himself (xliii. 13 ff., 25 ff.),
and so on. Sometimes, though surely less frequently,
it is possible that the narrators have invented new

scenes on the basis of the earlier motives, as with the last scene between Joseph and his brethren, chapter l.

Quite unique is the intercalated episode, the negotiations of Abraham with God regarding Sodom, which may almost be called a didactic composition. It is written to treat a religious problem which agitated the time of the author, and which occurred to him in connexion with the story of Sodom. These narrators have a quite remarkable fondness for long speeches, so great as to lead them to subordinate the action to the speeches. The most marked instance is the meeting of Abraham with Abimelech, chapter xx. Here, quite in opposition to the regular rule of ancient style, the events are not told in the order in which they occurred, but a series of occurrences are suppressed at the beginning in order to bring them in later in the succeeding speeches. Thus the narrator has attempted to make the speeches more interesting even at the expense of the incidents to be narrated.

It is also a favorite device to put substance into the speeches by having what has already been reported repeated by one of the personages of the story (xliii. 13, 21, 30 ff.; xliii. 3, 7, 20 f.; xliv. 19 ff). The rule of style in such repetition of speech is, contrary to the method of Homer, to vary them somewhat the second time. This preference for longer speeches is, as we clearly perceive, a secondary phenomenon in Hebrew style, the mark of a later period. We observe this in the fact that the very pieces which we recognise from other considerations as the latest developments of the legend or as intercalations (xiii. 14-17; xvi. 9 f.; xviii.

17-19, 23 - 33) are the ones which contain these speeches.

We may find this delight in discursiveness in other species of Hebrew literature also. The brief, condensed style of Amos is followed by the discursive style of a Jeremiah, and the same relation exists between the laconic sentences of the Book of the Covenant and the long-winded expositions of Deuteronomy, between the brief apothegms which constitute the heart of the Book of Proverbs and the extended speeches which were afterwards added by way of introduction, between the oldest folk-songs, which often contain but a single line each, and the long poems of art poetry.

INTEREST IN SOUL-LIFE.

We do not always agree with this taste of the later time; for instance, the story of Joseph approaches the danger-line of becoming uninteresting from excessive detail. On the other hand, this discursiveness is at the same time the evidence of a newly acquired faculty. While the earlier time can express its inner life only in brief and broken words, the new generation has learned to observe itself more closely and to express itself more completely. With this there has come an increase of interest in the soul-life of the individual. Psychological problems are now treated with fondness and with skill. Thus in the story of the sacrifice of Isaac there was created the perfection of the character study.

The narrator of the stories of Joseph shows himself a master of the art of painting the portrait of a man by means of many small touches. Especially suc-

cessful is the description of Joseph's inner vacilla-
tion at the sight of Benjamin (xliii. 30), and the
soul painting when Jacob hears that Joseph is still
alive (xlv. 26), and elsewhere. But while in these
later narratives the incidental features of the old
legend are still developed with greater detail, on
the other hand this very fact has naturally thrown
the chief features somewhat into the background
and made the original point of the whole less
obvious. This result has been further favored by
the circumstance that the original points had in
many cases ceased to be altogether clear to those
of the later time. Thus in the story of Joseph the
historical and ætiological elements have lost importance.

The difference between the two styles is so great
that it seems advisable to distinguish them by
different names, and to limit the use of "legend" to
the first while we call the second "romance." Of
course, the transition between the two is fluctuant;
we may call such transition forms as the story of
Laban and Jacob, or that of Rebeccah, "legends
touched with romance," or "romances based on
legendary themes."

On the relative age of these styles, also, an opinion may be ventured, though with great caution.
The art of narrative which was acquired in the writing of legends was applied later to the writing of
history, where, accordingly, we may make parallel
observations. Now we see that the oldest historical
writing known to us has already adopted the
"detailed" style. Accordingly we may assume that
this "detailed" style was cultivated at least as early
as the beginning of the time of the kings. And

therefore the condensed style must have been cultivated for many centuries before that time. However, it should be observed, this fixes only the
time of the styles of narrative, and not the age of
the narratives preserved to us in these styles.

IV.

HISTORY OF THE DEVELOPMENT OF THE LEGENDS OF GENESIS IN ORAL TRADITION.

A T the time when they were written down the legends were already very old and had already a long history behind them. This is in the very nature of legend: the origin of legends always eludes the eye of the investigator, going back into prehistoric times. And so it is in the present case. The great age of the legends is seen, for example, in the fact that they often speak of vanished tribes, such as Abel and Cain, Shem, Ham and Japhet, Jacob and Esau, none of which are known to historical times, and further, by the primitive vigor of many touches that reveal to us the religion and the morality of the earliest times, as for instance, the many mythological traces, such as the story of the marriages with angels, of Jacob's wrestling with God, and the many stories of deceit and fraud on the part of the patriarchs, and so on.

FOREIGN INFLUENCES.

A portion of these legends, perhaps very many, did not originate in Israel, but were carried into Israel from foreign countries. This too is part of the nature of these stories, this wandering from tribe to tribe, from land to land, and also from religion to religion. Thus for instance many of our German legends and *Märchen* came to us from foreign lands. And even to this day there is perhaps nothing which modern civilised peoples exchange so easily and so extensively as their stories, as may be seen, for instance, in the enormous circulation of foreign novels in Germany.

Now if we recall that Israel lived upon a soil enriched by the civilisation of thousands of years, that it lived by no means in a state of isolation but was surrounded on all sides by races with superior culture, and if we consider further the international trade and intercourse of the early ages, which went from Babylonia to Egypt and from Arabia to the Mediterranean by way of Palestine, we are warranted in assuming that this position of Israel among the nations will be reflected in its legends as well as in its language, which must be literally full of borrowed words.

Investigators hitherto, especially Wellhausen and his school, have erred frequently in assuming that the history of Israel could be interpreted almost exclusively from within, and in ignoring altogether too much the lines which connect Israel with the rest of the world. Let us trust that the investigators of the future will be more disposed than has hitherto been the case to give the history of Israel its place in the history of the world! Of course, with our slender knowledge of the primitive Orient we are in large measure thrown back upon conjectures. Yet this cannot justify us in ignoring altogether the surroundings in which Israel lived, and there are after all certain things which we may declare with tolerable certainty.

BABYLONIAN INFLUENCES.

Babylonian influence is evident more than any other in the primitive legends. We can demonstrate this in the case of the legend of the Deluge, of which we possess the Babylonian version; and we have strong reasons for accepting it in the case of the story of creation, which agrees with the Babylonian story in the characteristic point of the division of the primeval sea into two portions; also in the legend of Nimrod, and in the traditions of the patriarchs, the ten patriarchs of the race as given by P being ultimately the same as the ten primitive kings of the Babylonians. The legend of the Tower of Babel, too, deals with Babylonia and must have its origin in that region. The Eranian parallels to the legend of Paradise show that this, too, came from further East, but whether from Babylonia specifically is an open question, since the Babylonians located Paradise not at the source of the streams, so far as we know, but rather at their mouth. We have besides a Buddhistic parallel to the story of Sodom. (Cp. T. Cassel, *Mischle Sindbad.*)

As to the time when these legends entered Israel the opinions of investigators are divided; to us it seems probable from interior evidence that these legends wandering from race to race reached Canaan as early as some time in the second millennium B. C. and were adopted by Israel just as it was assimilating the civilisation of Canaan. We know from the Tell-el-Amarna correspondence that Babylonian influence was working upon Canaan even in this early period; and on the other hand, a later time,

when Israel's self-consciousness had awakened,
would scarcely have accepted these foreign myths.

EGYPTIAN AND PHŒNICIAN INFLUENCES.

Egyptian influence is recognisable in the romance
of Joseph, which has its scene partly in Egypt and
very likely goes back to Egyptian legends. This is
particularly evident in the legend of Joseph's
agrarian policy, xlvii. 13 ff. We may well wonder
that we find so few Egyptian elements in Genesis,
but so far as we can see the same observation is to be
made for the civilisation of Israel in general: Egypt
was already a decadent nation and had but slight
influence upon Canaan. We shall find also Phœni-
cian and Aramaic elements in the legends; the
second is proven by the importance of the city of
Haran to the patriarchs.

The probable home of the Ishmael legend is
Ishmael, and that of Lot the mountains of Moab,
where Lot's cave was shown, xix. 30. The Jacob-
Esau stories and the Jacob-Laban stories were originally told in "Jacob"; the Shem - Japhet - Canaan
legend in "Shem," as it would seem; the Abel-Cain
legend neither in Abel, which perished according to
the legend, nor in Cain, which was cursed and
exiled; accordingly in some unnamed people.

RELIGIOUS LEGENDS NOT ISRAELITIC.

The legends of worship in Genesis we may assume
with the greatest certainty to have originated in the
places of which they treat. The same may be said
of other legends which ascribe names to definite
places. Accordingly it is probable that most of the
legends of the patriarchs were known before Israel

came into Canaan. This assumption is supported
by the character of many of the legends of Genesis:
the complaisance and peacefulness of the figures of
the patriarchs are by no means Israelitish characteristics. The connexion of man and fruitland
(Cp. the *Commentary*, p. 5) in the story of Paradise
is conceivable only among a people of peasants.
According to the Cain and Abel legend also, the
field is God's property, iv. 14.

But especially the religion of Genesis hints of a
non-Israelitish origin for most of the legends: two
of our sources (E and P) avoid calling the God of
the patriarchs "Jahveh," in which we may see a last
relic of the feeling that these stories really have
nothing to do with "Jahveh" the God of Israel, as
furthermore the book of Job, which also treats a
foreign theme, does not use the name "Jahveh."
But even in the third source (J), which speaks of
"Jahveh," the name "Jahveh Zebaoth" is not
found. On a few occasions we are able to catch the
name of the pre-Jahvistic God of the legend; we
hear of "El Lahai Ro'i" at Lahai Ro'i, xvi. 30, of
"El 'Olam" at Beersheba, xxi. 33 ff., of "El
Bethel" at Bethel, xxxi. 13; El Shaddai and El
'Eljon are probably also such primitive names. In
the legend of Abraham at Hebron there are assumed
at the start three gods; polytheism is also to be
traced in the legend of the heavenly ladder at
Bethel and in the fragment of the Mahanaim
legend, xxxii. 2, where mention is made of many
divine beings.

We recognise Israelitish origin with perfect certainty only in those legends that introduce expressly
Israelitish names, that is particularly in the legends

of Dinah (Simeon and Levi) xxxiv, Tamar (Judah) xxxviii, and Reuben xxxv. 22. But we do not mean to declare by this that other narratives may not be of Israelitish origin. In particular the considerable number of legends which have their scene in Negeb (southward of Judah) may very likely be of Israelitish origin. But Israelitish tradition flows unmixed, so far as we can see, only from the introduction of the story of Moses.

The general view of the legendary traditions of Israel gives us, then, so far as we are able to make it out, the following main features: The legends of the beginnings in the main are Babylonian, the legends of the patriarchs are essentially Canaanitish, and after these come the specifically Israelitish traditions. This picture corresponds to the history of the development of civilisation: in Canaan the native civilisation grows up on a foundation essentially Babylonian, and after this comes the Israelitish national life. It is a matter of course that the sequence of periods in the themes for story-telling and in the epochs of civilisation should correspond; thus among modern peoples the children make the acquaintance first of the Israelitish stories, next of the Græco-Roman, and finally the modern subjects, quite in accordance with the influences in the history of our civilisation.

GREEK PARALLELS.

A particularly interesting problem is offered by the correspondence of certain legends to Greek subjects; for instance the story of the three men who visit Abraham is told among the Greeks by Hyrieus at Tanagra (Ovid, *Fast.*, V., 495 ff.); the story of

Potiphar's wife contains the same fictional motive
as that of Hippolytus and Phædra and is found in
other forms; there are also Greek parallels for the
story of the curse upon Reuben (Homer, *Iliad*, IX.,
447 ff.) and for the story of the quarrel of the
brothers Esau and Jacob (Apollodor., *Biblioth.*, II.,
2/1); the legend of Lot at Sodom suggests that of
Philemon and Baucis.   In the legends of the beginnings also there are related features: the declaration
that man and woman were originally one body
(Plato, *Symp.*, p. 189 ff.), and the myth of the
Elysian happiness of the primeval time are also
familiar to the Greeks. The solution of this problem will surely be found in the assumption that both
these currents of tradition are branches of one great
Oriental stream.

Accordingly we infer that the legends of Genesis
are of very varied origin, which is altogether confirmed by more careful examination. For the narratives themselves are far from consistent: some
conceive of the patriarchs as peasants, others as
shepherds, but never as city-dwellers; some have
their scene in Babylonia, some in Egypt, some in
Aram, and others in North and South Canaan; some
assume an original polytheism, others speak of the
guardian genius (El) of the place, some think of
God as the severe lord of mankind, others praise
the mercy of God, and so on.

THE ADAPTATION OF THE LEGENDS.

Naturally these foreign themes were vigorously
adapted in Israel to the nationality and the religion
of the people, a process to be recognised most
clearly in the case of the Babylonian-Hebrew legend

of the Deluge.   Here the polytheism has disappeared: the many gods have been dropped in favor
of the one (the myth of creation), or have been
reduced to servants of the one (the legend of
Hebron); the local divinities have been identified
with Jahveh and their names regarded as epithets of
Jahveh in the particular locality involved (xvi. 13;
xxi. 33; xxxi. 13).

The amalgamation of these legends and their
infilling with the spirit of a higher religion is one
of the most brilliant achievements of the people of
Israel.   But quite apart from the religion, in this
Israelitising of the legends it is very certain that a
quantity of changes took place of which we can
survey only a small portion.   Foreign personages
were displaced by native ones: as for instance the
Hebrew Enoch took the place of the Babylonian
magician Enmeduranki, while the more familiar
Noah took the place of the hero in the Babylonian
account of the Deluge.   Thus also the Egyptian
stories found in the last of Genesis were transferred
to the Israelite figure of Joseph.   And thus in many
cases the stories which are now connected with
definite personages may not have belonged to
them originally.   Or again, native personages
were associated with the foreign ones: thus Esau-
Se'ir was identified with Edom, and Jacob with
Israel, and Abraham, Isaac and Jacob made to be
ancestors of the people of Israel.   Or foreign
legends were localised in the places of Canaan:
thus the story of the three visitors of Abraham,
which is known also to the Greeks, is localised at
Hebron; the legend of the vanished cities, which
even in the form preserved knows nothing of the

salt lake, beside the Dead Sea.   And in the process
various specifically Israelitish features have been
introduced into the legends, for instance, the
prophecies that Esau (Edom) would sometime
separate from Jacob (Israel), xxvii. 40; that Joseph
would receive Shechem, xlviii. 22; that Manasseh
would dwindle as compared with Ephraim.   In the
legend of Jacob and Laban the motive of the boundary treaty at Gilead is a later interpolation;   a
piece about the preservation of Zoar has been added
to the legend of Sodom.   The legends of worship
which were originally intended to explain the sanctity of the place, were transferred to Jahveh and to
the patriarch Jared and received the new point that
they were to explain why Jared had the right to
worship Jahveh at this place.

MODE OF AMALGAMATION.

Further alterations came about by exchange or
combination of local traditions.   We can imagine
that such things happened very frequently in connexion with travel, especially perhaps on the occasion of
the great pilgrimages to the tribal sanctuaries, and
by means of the class of travelling story-tellers.
Thus the legends travelled from place to place and
are told in our present form of the tradition regarding various places.   The story of Sodom and
Gomorrah was localised, as it seems, by another
tradition at Adma and Sebo'im (cp. my *Commentary*, p. 195).   According to another tradition a
similar legend was told in connexion with Gibeah
in Benjamin (Judges xix).   The rescue of Ishmael
was localised both in Lahai Roï and in Beersheba
(xxi. 14).   The meeting of Jacob and Esau on the

former's return was located at Mahanaim and at
Penuel on the Jabbok (in Northeastern Canaan),
where it seems originally not to belong, since Esau
is supposed to be located in Edom, south of Canaan.
The names of the patriarchs are given in connexion
with the most various places, all claiming to have
been founded by them; Abraham particularly in
Hebron, but also in Beersheba and elsewhere; Isaac
not only in Beersheba, but also in Mizpah (xxxi.
53); Jacob in Penuel, Bethel and Shechem. In which
of the places the figures were originally located we
are unable to say, nor whether Abraham or Isaac
was the original personage in the legend of Gerar.
These transformations are too old to be traced out
in detail. Wellhausen's conjecture (*Prolegomena*,
p. 323) that Abraham is probably the latest personage among the patriarchs, is untenable.

Then again, various legends have been combined
(see pp. 45 and 56), for instance, the stories of Paradise and of the creation as told by J, and the myth
of the creation and of the Elysian period as told
by P.

Or again, various different personages have grown
together: thus the figure of Noah in Genesis consists
of three originally different personages, the builder
of the ark, the vintager, and the father of Shem,
Ham and Japhet. In Cain we have combined the
different personages: (1) Cain, the son of the first
human couple, (2) Cain, the brother of Abel, (3)
Cain, the founder of cities. Jacob, according to
the legend of Penuel, is a giant who wrestles with
God himself; according to the Jacob-Esau stories he
is shrewd but cowardly, thus seeming to be an
entirely different person; probably the Jacob to

whom God reveals himself at Bethel is still a different person.

Incidentally to the joining together of the legends the pedigrees of the patriarchs were established: thus Abraham became the father of Isaac, and he in turn of Jacob; thus Ishmael was made a son of Abraham and Lot made his nephew, and so on. And the reasons for this are not at all clear. How old this pedigree may be we cannot tell. The amalgamation of the legends is a process which certainly was under way long before Israel was in Canaan; we can imagine that it proceeded with especial rapidity and thoroughness at the time when Israel was again gathering itself together as a nation under the first kings.

FIDELITY OF TRANSMISSION.

And not only from place to place, but also from age to age, do our legends wander. In general they are simply repeated, and often with what is to us an incredible fidelity,—perhaps only half understood or grown entirely unintelligible, and yet transmitted further! How faithfully the legends have been told we can learn by comparing the different variants of the same story, which, in spite of more or less deviation, agree nevertheless in the general plan and often even in the very words. Compare, for instance, the two variants of the legend of Rebeccah.

And yet even these faithfully told legends are subject to the universal law of change. When a new generation has come, when the outward conditions have changed or the thoughts of men have altered, whether it be in religion or ethical ideals or æsthetic taste, the popular legend cannot per-

manently remain the same. Slowly and hesitat-
ingly, always at a certain distance behind, the
legends follow the general changes in conditions,
some more, others less. And here, consequently,
the legends furnish us a very important basis for
judging of changes in the people; a whole history
of the religious, ethical and æsthetic ideas of
ancient Israel can be derived from Genesis.

VALUE OF THE VARIANTS.

If any one proposes to study this history he will
do well to begin with the variants. It is the characteristic of legend as well as of oral tradition that
it exists in the form of variants. Each one, however faithful it may be, and especially every particular group and every new age, tells somewhat
differently the story transmitted to it. The most
important variants in Genesis are the two stories of
Ishmael (xvi.; xxi. 8 ff.), and next the legend of
the danger to the patriarch's wife, which is handed
down to us in three versions (xii. 13 ff. xxvi. 7 *ff*),
and then the associated legend of the treaty at
Beersheba, likewise in three versions. In the case
of these stories the variants are told with almost
entire independence of one another.

To these are to be added the many cases in which
the stories are transmitted to us in the variants of J
and E (or of the various hands in J) worked over by
the hand of an editor; the chief illustrations of this
method being the stories of Jacob and of Joseph.
Sometimes, furthermore, variants of portions of
Genesis are transmitted to us in other Biblical
books: thus the idyllic account of the way in which
Jacob became acquainted with Rachel at the foun-

tain is told also of Moses and Zipporah; the renun-
ciation of the old gods under the oak at Shechem is
told of Jacob and also of Joshua (Joshua xxiv.); the
interpretation of the dream of the foreign king is
told of both Joseph and Daniel.

Let the investigator make his first observations
on these twice-told tales; when he has thus acquired
the keen eye and found certain lines of development, then let him compare also the legends which
are told but once. Then he will begin to see how
extraordinarily varied these legends are; among
them are the coarsest and the most delicate, the
most offensive and the most noble, those showing a
naïve, polytheistic religion, and others in which is
expressed the most ideal form of faith.

JUDGMENT OF INDIVIDUAL NARRATIVES.

Moreover, the history of the legends is to be
derived from the individual narratives themselves.
If we look sharply we shall see revisions in the taste
of a later time, slight or extensive additions bringing in a thought which was foreign to the old narrator; in certain rare cases we may even assume that
a whole story has been added to the tradition (chap.
xv.); and such additions are recognised by the fact
that they are out of place in an otherwise harmonious story, and usually also by the fact that they are
relatively unconcrete: the art of story-telling, which
in olden times was in such high perfection, degen-
erated in later times, and the latest, in particular,
care more for the thought than for the narrative.
Hence such additions usually contain speeches.
Sometimes also short narrative notes are added to
the legend cycles, as for instance, we are told briefly

of Jacob that he bought a field in Shechem (xxxiii. 18-20), or that Deborah died and was buried at Bethel (xxxv. 8), and so on.

But with these faithful narrators more significant than the additions are certainly the omissions which are intended to remove features that have become objectionable; for we find gaps in the narratives at every step. Indeed, to those of a later time often so much had become objectionable or had lost its interest that some legends have become mere torsos: such is the case with the marriages with angels, with the story of Reuben (xxxv. 21-22a), of Mahanaim (xxxiii. 2 ff.). In other cases only the names of the figures of the legend have come down to us without their legends: thus of the patriarchs Nahor, Iscah, Milcah (xi. 29), Phichol, Ahuzzath (xxvi. 26); from the legend of the giant Nimrod we have only the proverbial phrase, "like Nimrod, a mighty hunter before the Lord" (x. 9). By other instances we can see that the stories, or particular portions of them, have lost their connexion and were accordingly no longer rightly understood: the narrators do not know why Noah's dove brought precisely an olive leaf (viii. 11), why Judah was afraid to give to Tamar his youngest son also (xxxviii. 11), why Isaac had but one blessing to give (xxvii. 36), and why he had to partake of good things before the blessing (xxvii. 4), why it was originally told that Jacob limped at Penuel (xxxii. 32), and so forth.

Hence there is spread over many legends something like a blue haze which veils the colors of the landscape: we often have a feeling that we indeed are still able to recall the moods of the ancient legends, but that the last narrators had ceased to have a true appreciation of those moods. We must pursue all these observations, find the reasons that led to the transformations, and thus describe the inner history of the legends. But here we give only a short sketch.

CHANGES WROUGHT BY TIME IN THE LEGENDS.

The most important element in the history of the legends is probably this: in older times as the outward circumstances in which they arose were shifted, the legends also incurred certain alterations. Thus it was forgotten who the king of Gerar really was (xx. 26), and the king of Egypt was put in instead (xii. 10 ff.). Incidentally it seems, according to Winckler, that a confusion arose between Mizraim (Egypt) and the North Arabian tribe of the Muzrim, to whom Gerar belonged; and Hagar also has been changed from a Muzritish Arabian woman to a woman of Mizraim, that is, an Egyptian. Or, at a time when the Philistines had possession of Gerar this people also was brought into the legend of Gerar, whereas the oldest version of the story (xxi. 22 ff., 26) knows as yet nothing of this fact. The figure of Hagar, once the type of a tempestuous Bedouin woman (xvi.) has lost this characteristic color in the later tradition, which was not familiar with the desert. The stories of Jacob's breeding devices while in Laban's employ, once the delight of the professional hearers and therefore quite detailed, were later much abbreviated for hearers or readers who had no interest in the subject. (See *Commentary*, p. 307.) Of the theories regarding the gradual origin of human arts and trades (iv. 17 ff.) only fragments have been preserved. Very often the characteristic elements of the legend, when far from the places where they were understood, grew colorless or were replaced by others. This is particularly clear in the legends of sanctuaries, of which we shall speak later. Still other legends were probably entirely forgotten because the interest in them had died out. And in addition to this, the imagination, which is mightily stirred by such narratives, develops them almost involuntarily. We can here and there recognise such continuations and developments due to the free play of the imagination.

LIGHT ON THE HISTORY OF RELIGION.

The most important feature of this study is the history of religion. In very many legends of Genesis a monotheistic tendency is to be observed, an avoidance of mythology to which we have referred (see pp. 15 and 95). This feeling continued to grow in Israel and was the cause for the fading out of a number of legends. In the case of the myth of creation, of which we have older variants of a different attitude, the history of this elimination of the mythological elements is still to be observed. The narrative of the Deluge, too, has lost much of its color in the oldest Hebrew account (that of J), and doubtless from this very reason. Others, like the legend of the marriage with angels (vi. 1-4) and of Mahanaim (xxxv. 21-22*a*), which were once in existence in older Israelitish tradition, are in their present form entirely mutilated. Of the Nephilim, the Hebrew "Titans," which are said to have been very famous once (vi. 4), we have nothing but the name.

MODIFICATION OF THE THEOPHANY.

Furthermore, we may observe how naïvely the older legends speak of Jahveh's appearance on earth, but how the later time objected to this and made the revelation of the divinity even more intangible. While according to the oldest belief the divinity himself walked without reserve among men—as in the present form of the legends of Paradise and of the Deluge—the later time decked the theophany in the veil of mystery: God appeared only in the darkness of night and vanished with the rising of the sun (xix.); or he appeared to men without their recognising him (xviii.), and in this way the divinity, though revealing himself, nevertheless did not wholly unveil his nature. Still later versions put some subordinate divine being in place of the divinity himself, J calling it "the angel of Jahveh," and E "the angel of God," though this device was not observed consistently; passages enough have been left which presuppose the appearance of Jahveh himself, the older version peeping forth from behind the newer one.

This same point of view has led to the change of God's appearance on earth to the apparition in a dream, or to the declaration that the angel remained in heaven and spoke to the patriarch from there: the mystery of the dream-life left a veil for the divinity who revealed himself, or in the other case he was not seen at all, but only heard. The last stage in this development is represented by those legends in which the divinity no longer appears at a definite point in the story, but dominates the whole from the ultimate hidden background, as in the stories of Rebeccah and of Joseph.

Thus we progress in Genesis by many stages from crass mythology to a belief in providence which seems to us altogether modern. It is a marvel indeed that the legend of Penuel (xxxii. 25 ff.) is transmitted to us in such primitive form; in this the device has been to leave it undefined who the God really was that attacked Jacob.

THE DIVINITY AND THE SANCTUARY.

We recognise in this process of refining the nature of the theophany at the same time the dissociation of the divinity from the sanctuaries: the oldest belief that the God belonged to this particular place and could operate nowhere else, is not clearly found in a single legend of Genesis. On the contrary, the opinion of the legend is that the places are sacred to the divinity because he had once in primitive time appeared here to some ancestor. Even the very old legend of Hebron, which actually has God appear and eat, does not allege that the divinity came forth out of the tree. In the story of Hagar's flight, the mother of Ishmael meets the divinity at the well, but no explanation is given as to what connexion he had with the well. The great age of this whole point of view is to be gathered from the story of Bethel: the oldest religion had thought to find the God of the place in the stone itself, as the name of the sacred stone, *beth-el*, or "house of God," shows; but those of the later age believed that God dwelt high above Bethel, in heaven, and only a ladder preserved the connexion between the real dwelling of God and its symbol. This belief in the heavenly dwelling of the divinity rested, as the legend shows, upon a polytheistic basis: Jacob sees many divine beings going up and down the ladder.

Many legends of sanctuaries are transmitted to us in very faded form: from the story of Ishmael (in both versions) and likewise from the legends of Hebron (xviii.), Mahanaim (xxxii. 2 f.), Penuel (xxxii. 25 ff.) and others, we no longer gather that the scenes of the stories are places of worship. The legend of the sacrifice of Isaac, originally a legend of worship, has lost all its ætiological purpose in the version transmitted to us and remains nothing but a character sketch. In the legend of Penuel, too, the ætiological element is now forgotten. The anointing of the stone at Bethel, once a sacrificial ceremony, seems in its transmitted form to be no more than a sort of rite of consecration. The Massëbhâ, once sacred stones, symbols of the divinity, are finally mere memorial or tomb stones. The cave of Machpelah, once a place of worship, is nothing but the burial-place of the patriarchs in our form of the narrative. And so on.

The fading out of these legends of worship shows plainly that these stories are not preserved for us in the form in which they were probably told originally on the spot for the purpose of establishing its sanctity, but as they circulated among the people in later times and far from the places concerned. At the same time we see from this colorless character of the legends concerning the popular sanctuaries that the latter had ceased to occupy the foreground of religious interest with the people, or at least with certain groups of the people. The bond between religion and the sanctuaries was already loosened when the passionate polemic of the prophets severed it. How else could the people of Judah have accepted the "Deuteronomian Reformation," which destroyed these places with the exception of the royal temple at Jerusalem! (2 Kings xxiii.).

GOD'S RELATION TO MAN.

Genesis furnishes the most varied utterances concerning the relation of the divinity to mankind. In the oldest legends we hear how God holds men in check, how he guards and favors certain individuals in accordance with his sovereign pleasure, and how he glorifies and aggrandises his people above all others. In certain of the oldest legends God's action in such cases seems not to involve at all any thought of the moral or religious attitude of men: God reveals himself to Jacob at Bethel simply because Jacob happens to come to Bethel; similarly at Penuel the divinity assails Jacob without any evident reason; God is pleased with Abel's offering simply because he loves Abel the shepherd; he protects Abraham in Egypt and gives a fortunate outcome to the patriarch's deception; in any conflict of the patriarch with third parties God takes the part of his favorite even when the latter is plainly in the wrong as in the case of Abraham in dealing with Abimelech (xx. 7), or when he has indulged in very questionable practises, as in the case of Jacob with Laban, and so on.

But alongside these there are other legends upon a higher plane, according to which God makes his favor to depend upon the righteousness of men: he destroys sinful Sodom, but saves Lot because of his hospitableness; he destroys the disobliging Onan, and exiles Cain because of his fratricide; Joseph is

helped by him because he has deserved assistance
by his chastity and his magnanimity; to Abraham
he gives a son because of his kindness to strangers.
These legends all belong, taken absolutely, to a
later time which has a finer ethical sense, yet they
are all primitive in Israel. The belief that God
looks with approval upon the just and rewards the
wicked according to his sin is certainly familiar to
the religion of Israel from the beginning (cp. 1 Sam.
xxiv. 20; 2 Sam. iii. 39). From a broader point of
view we may include here another group of legends
which tell how God has compassion on the outcast
and despairing; a particularly affecting instance of
this is the legend of the exile of Hagar (xxi. 8 ff.).

A third variety of legend emphasises strongly
what it is that wins God's approval, to wit, faith,
obedience, invincible trust,—these God imputes as
righteousness. At God's command Noah built a
ship upon dry land; following God's word Abraham
left his secure home and migrated to alien lands,
trusting in God's promise that he should become a
nation despite the fact that he had not even a son
as yet. Thus they won the favor of God. The
legend of the suit for the hand of Rebeccah also
shows how such steadfast trust in God is rewarded.
In the legend of the sacrifice of Isaac we have a
wonderful character sketch showing how the man of
true piety submits to even the hardest and most terrible trials if God so commands. The famous prayer
of Jacob, xxxii. 10-13, portrays the humble gratitude of the pious man who confesses himself to be
unworthy of the divine favor. The narratives and
pieces which speak thus of divine favor mark the
climax of high religious feeling in Genesis; it is

these especially which give value to Genesis even for the piety of the present day. We see in them a comparatively late development. This conclusion is supported by other reasons in the case of most of them: the Babylonian legend of the Deluge, for instance, knows nothing of the trial of the hero's faith; Jacob's prayer is quite secondary in its connexion, and what a contrast this prayer and its deep feeling makes with the remaining conduct of the eel-like Jacob! What a difference between it and the legend which stands beside it, Jacob's wrestling with the divinity! It is to be noted also how peculiarly inconcrete the story of Abraham's exodus is; while the narrative of the covenant, chapter xv., is perhaps a later composition without any basis of tradition!

NOT MERELY A TRIBAL GOD.

Thus we can discern here a series of thoughts about God leading from the crudest up to the highest. But in any case these legends teach that it is an error to think that ancient Israel conceived only of a relation between God and Israel; on the contrary, it is everywhere a matter of the relation of God to individual men. It is true that these persons are in part race types, but the legend looks upon them as persons and depicts God's relation to them in large measure just in the way in which the people of that time believed that God dealt with individuals. We should deprive many of these narratives of their whole charm if we failed to recognise this fact: the reason the legend of Hebron was heard so gladly by ancient listeners is that it tells how God rewards hospitality (thine and mine

also!); and the story of how God hears the voice of
the weeping boy Ishmael in the wilderness is touching because it shows God having compassion on
a child: this God will hear the cry of our children
also!

RELIGIOUS AND PROFANE MOTIVES MINGLED.

Another line of development is seen in the fact
that the elder stories have a naïve way of mingling
profane and religious motives, and clearly without
taking any offence at it: thus the legend of Abraham in Egypt celebrates the shrewdness of the
patriarch, the beauty of his wife and the steadfast-
ness of God. The legend of the Deluge praises not
only the piety, but also the shrewdness, of Noah
(in the story of his sending out the birds); the
legend of the flight of Hagar (xvi.) gives quite a
realistic picture of the condition of affairs in Abraham's household and then tells of God's assistance.
These legends come, therefore, from a time when
profane and sacred matters were still frankly united,
when the men of Israel fought at the same time for
God and the popular hero ("a sword for Jahveh and
Gideon!" Judges vii. 20), when lively humor was
not inconsistent with piety, as, for instance, the
merry butcher Samson who is at the same time
God's *nazir* (devotee), or the humor of the legend
of Abraham in Egypt. Now we see by the variants
especially of this last legend that later times no
longer tolerated this mingling of profane and sacred
motives, or at least that it offended by the attempt
to glorify at the same time God and profane qualities of men. Accordingly this later time constructed stories which are specifically "sacred,"

that is, which deal only with God and piety, and in which profane interests are relegated to the background. Such legends are those of Abraham's exodus, of the covenant, of the sacrifice of Isaac, and so on. Here the formerly popular saga is on the point of becoming "legend," that is, a characteristically "sacred" or "priestly" narrative. Whether this phenomenon was connected with the fact that the legends were at that time making their way into certain definite "sacred" or "priestly" circles, we are unable to say.

The earlier times knew also legends of the patriarchs which were altogether of profane character, such as the legend of the separation of Abraham and Lot, or that of Jacob and Laban. In later tradition religious elements made their way into even these legends and gave them a religious coloring. For instance, objection was taken to the notion that Canaan belonged to Abraham simply because Lot did not choose it, and an addition supplied to the effect that God himself after Lot's withdrawal personally promised the land to Abraham (xiii. 14-17). Similarly, later narrators hesitated to say that Jacob had run away from Laban and accordingly interpolated the explanation that God had revealed the plan to him (xxxi. 3).

ETHICAL NOTIONS IN THE LEGENDS.

Furthermore, a whole history of ethics can be constructed from these legends. Many of the legends of the patriarchs are filled with the pure enjoyment of the characters of the patriarchs. Consequently many things in these characters which are to us

offensive caused no hesitation in the time which
first told the stories, but were, on the contrary, a
source of pleasure or of inspiration.   The people of
old took pleasure in Benjamin's career of plunder
(xlix. 29), in Hagar's defiant spirit (xvi.) and in
the courage of Tamar and the daughters of Lot, who
took seed of a man where they could find it, and
further in the shrewd deceit of Abraham in Egypt,
in Joseph's cunning when he introduced his brothers to his prince as shepherds (xlvii. 1 f.), in
Rachel's trick by which she deceived her father so
perfectly (xxxi. 34), and especially in the wiles and
schemes of the arch-rogue Jacob.   It is impossible
to ignore the great rôle played by deceit and cunning in these legends of the patriarchs, and the
amusement the people of old got out of it, and the
character which they thus reveal to us.   Then we
see from many examples how the later tradition
took offence at these stories, re-interpreted them or
remodeled them and tried to eliminate the questionable features as far as this was possible.   This
is most evident in the variants of the legend of the
danger of Sarah: here the later narrators have
remodeled the whole story, which plainly appeared
highly questionable to them, changing, for instance,
Abraham's lie into a mental reservation (xx. 12),
the disgraceful presents which the patriarch receives
for his wife into a testimonial of good repute (xx.
16), and even finally deriving Abraham's wealth
from the blessing of God (xxvi. 12); similarly, the
deportation of Abraham (xii. 20) has been changed
into its opposite (xx. 15), and so on.

The defiant Hagar of chapter xvi. has been
changed into a patient and unfortunate woman, in

order that no offence might be taken with God's
compassion upon her (xxi. 8 ff.); the attempt has
been made to explain Abraham's treatment of
Hagar by adding that God had commanded him to
put her away (xxi. 11). Especial pains has been
taken to clear Jacob of the charge of dishonesty in
his relations with Laban: in several long speeches
the narrator undertakes the demonstration that
there is no shadow upon Jacob; Jacob's wives and
finally Laban himself are obliged to recognise his
uprightness (xxxi. 4 ff.; 36 ff.). Here too the resort
is, to ascribe to the authority of God that which
seems questionable to men: God always caused the
herds to bring forth in Jacob's interest (xxxi. 7),
and God himself revealed to Jacob the color of the
newborn for the coming year (xxxi. 10 ff.). With
somewhat less energy the narrators have taken hold
of the story of Tamar; yet here too they have done
their best to wash Judah white: Judah, they urge,
did not go to Timnath until his wife was dead.
And a similar endeavor has been made to give at
least for Lot himself a somewhat more decent shape
to the story of Lot's daughters, which was very
offensive to those of the later age: they say that
Lot was deceived by his daughters.

THE PATRIARCHS NOT SAINTS.

The olden time undoubtedly took delight in the
patriarchs; it did not consider them saints, but told
of them quite frankly all sorts of things that were
far from ideal. Some of the old stories are in this
respect exceedingly true to nature: they portray
the fathers as types of the Israelitish nationality

just such as individual men in Israel are. Thus the story of the flight of Hagar (xvi.) sketches the people in Abraham's household: Sarah as the jealous wife, Hagar as the defiant slave, and Abraham as the peace-loving husband. The later time with its "sacred" or "priestly" feeling could not tolerate such things. On the contrary, this age always saw in the patriarchs models of piety, and of that intense and tender piety which belonged to this later age. Thus there has entered into the portraits of the patriarchs a peculiar dissonance: the very Abraham who thrust his son Ishmael into the wilderness (xxi. 14), who does not hesitate to turn Sarah over to the foreign king and even to accept presents for her (xii. 16), we are asked to regard as the same who is the lofty model of faith for all ages! And the cunning Jacob is the same who speaks the wonderful prayer of gratitude! We resolve this dissonance and free these legends from the unpleasant suspicion of untruthfulness by recognising that the different tones are the product of different periods.

The earlier time did not hesitate to recognise here and there the rights of aliens when brought into conflict with the patriarchs: for instance, Pharaoh's right as opposed to Abraham's (xii. 18 f.), and Esau's as opposed to Jacob's (xxvii. 36); indeed some of the patriarchs have been simply abandoned: Simeon, Levi and Reuben were cursed by their great-grandfather (xlix. 3-7)! Israelitish patriotism was at that time so sound that it tolerated such views. But the later times, with their one-sided, excessive reverence for "the people of God," could not endure the thought that the patriarchs

had ever been wrong or done wrong. Thus we see
how one of the narrators takes pains to show that
Abraham was not altogether in the wrong in his
relations with Abimelech (in the speech, xxi. 11-13).
From the same motive, in order to avoid saying
anything bad about the patriarchs, only a fragment
of the story of the curse of Reuben has been transmitted (xxxv. 21-22a), and the story of Simeon and
Levi has been cast into several forms (xxxiv.): first
excuses for the brothers were sought—they were
defending the honor of their sister(J)—and finally
they were even justified and their betrayal of
Shechem represented as quite the natural thing.
Here, too, God is finally made to take their side
(E, cp. xxxv. 5). We do not always relish such
modifications, and sometimes it seems to us as if
they made the matter worse, rather than better.
Thus, the lie of Abraham in introducing his wife as
his sister (xii. 13), in which the earlier narrators
take evident pleasure, is after all more tolerable
than the mental reservation which is put in its place,
which seems to us Jesuitical (xx. 12). But despite
these instances we must not surrender our gratifica-
tion at this gradual improvement in ethical judgment which we can see in Genesis.

On the history of ethical taste which is to be
found in these legends we have already treated in
the preceding pages (see p. 111) and have but a few
points to add here. We gain a deep insight into
the heart of the primitive people when we collect
the chief motives in which the eye of the legends
takes pleasure. This is not the place for such a
summary; attention may, however, be called to the
fact of how little is said of murder and assassina-

tion, and on the contrary how much is said of peaceful occupations and household affairs, especially of the begetting of children; eating and drinking, too, play quite a rôle. These narrators are thoroughly posted in the life of peasants and shepherds and are therefore a prime source for our "archæology"; but they are not at home in political affairs: in this they are simple and natural.

The older legends are often quite coarse: for instance, the legend of the defiant Hagar (xvi.), or Jacob's deception of his blind father and the delight of the listeners (xxvii.), or the exceedingly coarse way in which Laban's quick-witted daughter deceives her father (xxxi. 34 f.): it must have been a strong, coarse race that took pleasure in such stories. How very different are the later stories which overflow with tears, such as the legend of the exile of Hagar (xxi.), of the sacrifice of Isaac, and especially the legends of Joseph! Here a different generation is expressing itself, one that loves emotion and tears.

Still another distinction between the older and the later time is that the former was interested in the familiar things of its nearest surroundings, while the latter tries to give a piquant charm to its stories by locating the legend far away and introducing the description of foreign customs, as in the story of Joseph.

CRITERIA OF THE AGE OF THE LEGENDS.

Accordingly we have an abundance of grounds on which we can establish the age or the youth of the narratives. Sometimes we are enabled to outline a very brief preliminary or pre-natal history of the legend in question, as for instance in the case of the legend of Hagar (xvi.), in which first an "El," then Jahveh himself, and then his messenger, was the divinity that appeared. Often a series of various arguments lead to a given conclusion, that a legend is late or early; thus the legend of Abraham in Egypt is to be regarded for many reasons as very old; it is very brief, has a primitive local coloring, and does not idealise its personages, and so on. On the other hand, many arguments lead to the conclusion that the legend of Joseph is very late: it has the latest, spun-out style, few ætiological elements, contains the belief in Providence, and so on. But very often the various considerations cross one another: in that case it is evident that the legend contains a confused mixture of early and late elements: thus the narrative in chapter xv., containing no complications, seems to be relatively late, but the theophany in fire and smoke is surely a very primitive conception. The different phases of development have not been distinct and clear cut: early features often continued to hold their own for a long time; hence it will be necessary to conceive of this outline of the history of the legends not as simple and straightforward, but as very confused and full of vicissitudes.

TRIBAL LEGENDS.

If we take one more survey of the history of these transformations, we shall surely have to admit that we can get sight of only a small part of the entire process. These transmutations must have begun at a very early period, a period so early that our sources give us no insight into it. This should warn us against supposing that we are able to arrive always at the very primitive significance of the stories from the historical and ætiological allusions which we find in the narratives. In this connexion we may refer to the legends in which there have been no such allusions from the beginning, especially the legend of Jacob and Laban. And a special warning is needed against rashly interpreting as tribal legends those legends whose heroes are plainly ancestors of tribes, for it may be, as has been shown above, that the story was applied to the tribal hero long after its origin.

And if it is scarcely possible for us to declare from the sources handed down to us the original significance of the legends, neither may we claim to know in every case who the originals were of the figures in the legends of the patriarchs. Some of them are really names of countries, or races, and of tribes, as for instance, Israel, Ishmael, Ammon, Moab, Rachel, Leah, Hagar, Keturah, and the tribes of Israel. In an inscription of Thotmosis III (ca. 1500 B. C.) mention is made of a Canaanitish tribe or district J'qb'ar, which would correspond to a Hebrew Ja'ᵃqob'el (Hebrew l = Egyptian r); and the name Jacob-el would be related to Jacob as Jephthahel and Jabnᵃel are related to Jephthah and Jabne: they are all names of tribes or of places, like Israel, Ishmael, and Jᵉrahmᵉel. Even on this evidence we should conclude that Jacob was originally the name of a Canaanitish district, which existed in Canaan before the Israelitish immigration.[1]

---

[1] Cp. Ed. Meyer ZAW 1886, p. 1. ff.

PATRIARCHS DISGUISED DIVINITIES.

Still another question is, whether these tribal names were not also originally names of divinities, as for instance Asshur is at the same time the name of the God of Asshur (Assyria). This is to be assumed for Gad, which is at the same time the name of the god of fortune, and also for Edom— cp. the name Obed-edom, "servant of Edom." [1] Names of divinities have been suspected further in Selah (cp. the name Methuselah = man of Selah), Re'u (cp. the name Re'u-el), Nahor (cp. the name Ebednahor = servant of Nahor), Terah (perhaps the same as the North-Syrian god Tarhu), Haran (cp. the name Bethharan = temple of Haran). Sarah and Milkah are, as we know, names of the goddesses of Haran, with which the Biblical figures of Sarah and Milkah have perhaps some connexion. This suggests very easily the thought that Abraham, the husband of Sarah, has been substituted for the (moon-) god of Haran. The name Laban, too, suggests a god: Le bana means moon; the fact that Laban is represented as being a shepherd would correspond to his character as a moon-god: for the moon-god may be represented as the shepherd of the clouds. In ancient as well as in modern times the attempt has been repeatedly made to explain the figures of Abraham, Isaac, and Jacob also as originally gods. There is no denying that this conjecture is very plausible. The whole species of the legend—though not indeed every individual legend —originated in the myth; at least many legends are derived from myths. And such an interpreta-

---

[1] Wellhausen Composition[2], p. 47, 2. ed.

tion is very natural for the stories of Jonah in the whale's belly, of Esther (Istar), of Samson (Semes's sun) and others. What is more natural than to attempt this interpretation with the legends of Genesis whose origin goes back in part to prehistoric times when myths were the order of nature? But— as we look at it—the attempts in this line hitherto made have not been exactly fortunate and have sometimes failed to demonstrate their theses. Of such pieces as can be interpreted with reasonable certainty as remnants of mythical narratives there are not many among the tales of the patriarchs (we are not now speaking of the legends of the beginnings): the note that Abraham with 318 servants slew his enemies (xiv. 14) may, in Winckler's opinion, go back to a moon-myth, the moon being visible 318 days in the year; Jacob's wrestling with God suggests that this Jacob was really a Titan, and consequently we can scarcely avoid seeing here a faded out myth; Joseph's dream that the sun, the moon, and eleven stars were compelled to bow down before him must have been originally an oracle referring to the Lord of Heaven before whom the highest powers of heaven bow, although it seems that this dream was introduced very late into the story of Joseph.

CAUTION NEEDED IN INTERPRETATION.

But before we are warranted in declaring with regard to a figure in Genesis that it bears the impress of an earlier god, we must demand not merely that certain elements of a story *permit* a mythical interpretation, but that whole legends shall possess striking resemblances to known myths, or that they can be interpreted as myths in perfectly clear and unquestioned fashion. Such a demonstration as this has not been given by investigators hitherto.[1] Let us hope that those who attempt it in the future may be more successful! But let us by no means fail to recognise the fact that Israel in historical times, when these legends were told, saw in Abraham, Isaac, and Jacob, not gods but men, its ancestors. And we must further demand that

---

[1] The older theory of Goldziher (*Der Mythos bei den Hebräern*, 1876), which depended chiefly on the etymologies of names, is long since discredited. Stucken (*Astralmythen*, I. Abraham, 1896, II. Lot, 1897) bases his assertions upon individual elements of the legends, for which he hunts together an amazing abundance of parallels from all over the world; but these parallels are often only very incidental. As Etana, carried up to heaven by an eagle, according to the Babylonian myth, looks down upon the earth, so Abraham and Lot, according to Stucken, look upon the land from Bethel, and so Abraham looks up to heaven and upon Sodom. But such analogies will not stand attack. Winckler, *Geschichte Israels*, II., 1900, who continues to build upon this uncertain foundation, depends especially upon the characteristic numbers: the four wives of Jacob are the four phases of the moon, his twelve sons the months; the seven children of Leah are the gods of the days of the week, the 300 pieces of silver which Benjamin, the youngest, receives are the 30 days of the last month, the 5 state dresses are the 5 intercalary days; Joseph's coat suggests the garments of Tamar and Istar (and every other garment!); his being thrown into the cistern denotes the descent of Tammuz into the under world; the dipping of his coat in blood and his father's belief that he had been eaten by a wild beast suggest the slaying of Adonis by the boar, and so on. After such a review we cannot yet see satisfactory solutions of the problem in either of these works, although we gladly recognize the extensive learning and the keenness of them both. And yet we would emphasize the point, that there is no reason on principle against a mythical interpretation of the legends of the patriarchs.

those investigators who propose to find mythological foundations to our legends must first of all inves-
tigate most carefully the history of the legends
which lies before us so clearly in the sources. Only
for the oldest elements of the legends may a mythical origin be ultimately expected. Accordingly we
are unable to say what the figures of Abraham,
Isaac, and Jacob, which chiefly interest us, may
have signified originally. But this is by no means
strange. These matters are simply too primitive
for us.

Meditative apologetics is wont to lay great importance upon the historical verity of Abraham; in our
opinion there is no longer any room for this
assumption, and moreover it is hard to see what
significance this position can have for religion and
the history of religion. For even if there had
once been a leader by the name of Abraham, as is
generally believed, and who conducted the migration from Haran to Canaan, this much is beyond
question with every one who knows anything of the
history of legends, that a legend cannot be expected
to preserve throughout so many centuries a picture
of the personal piety of Abraham. The religion of
Abraham is in reality the religion of the narrators
of the legends, ascribed by them to Abraham.

V.

JAHVIST, ELOHIST, JEHOVIST, THE LATER COLLECTIONS.

V.

JAHVIST, ELOHIST, JEHOVIST, THE LATER COLLECTIONS.

THE collecting of legends began even in the state of oral tradition. In the preceding pages (see p. 79 ff.) we have shown how individual stories first attracted one another and greater complexes of legends were formed. Connecting portions were also composed by these collectors, such, notably, as the story of the birth of the sons of Jacob, which is not at all a popular legend but the invention of older story-tellers, and must have been in existence even before the work of J and E. And there are further additions, such as the note that Jacob bought a field at Shechem, and other similar matters. Those who first wrote down the legends continued this process of collection. The writing down of the popular traditions probably took place at a period which was generally disposed to authorship and when there was a fear that the oral traditions might die out if they were not reduced to writing. We may venture to conjecture that the guild of story-tellers had ceased to exist at that time, for reasons unknown to us. And in its turn the reduction to writing probably contributed to kill out the remaining remnants of oral tradition, just as the written law destroyed the institution of the priestly Thora, and the New Testament canon the primitive Christian Pneumatics.

The collection of the legends in writing was not done by one hand or at one period, but in the course of a very long process by several or many hands. We distinguish two stages in this process: the older, to which we owe the collections of the Jahvist designated by 'J' and the Elohist designated by 'E', and then a later, thorough revision in what is known as the Priestly Codex 'P'. In the preceding pages as a rule only those legends have been used which we attribute to J and E. All these books of legends contain not only the primitive legends, of which we have been speaking, but also tell at the same time their additional stories; we may (with Wildeboer) characterise their theme as "the choice of Israel to be the people of Jahveh"; in the following remarks, however, they will be treated in general only so far as they have to do with Genesis.

"JAHVIST" AND "ELOHIST" COLLECTORS, NOT AUTHORS.

Previous writers have in large measure treated J and E as personal authors, assuming as a matter of course that their writings, constitute, at least to some extent, units and originate in all essential features with their respective writers, and attempting to derive from the various data of these writings consistent pictures of their authors. But in a final phase criticism has recognised that these two collections do not constitute complete unities, and pursuing this line of knowledge still further has distinguished within these sources still other subordinate sources.[1]

But in doing this there has been a neglect to raise with perfect clearness the primary question, how far these two groups of writings may be understood as literary unities in any sense, or whether, on the contrary, they are not collections, codifications of oral traditions, and whether their composers are not to be called collectors rather than authors.

That the latter view is the correct one is shown (1) by the fact that they have adopted such heterogeneous materials. J contains separate legends and legend cycles, condensed and detailed stories, delicate and coarse elements, primitive and modern elements in morals and religion, stories with vivid antique colors along with those quite faded out. It is much the same with E, who has, for instance, the touching story of the sacrifice of Isaac and at the same time a variant of the very ancient legend of Jacob's wrestling with the angel. This variety shows that the legends of E, and still more decidedly those of J, do not bear the stamp of a single definite time and still less of a single personality, but that they were adopted by their collectors essentially as they were found.

Secondly, the same conclusion is suggested by an examination of the variants of J and of E. On the one hand they often agree most characteristically: both, for instance, employ the most condensed style in the story of Penuel, and in the story of Joseph the most detailed. For this very reason, because they are so similar, it was possible for a later hand to combine them in such a way that they are often

---

[1] Such is the outcome especially in Budde's *Urgeschichte.*

merged to a degree such that it is impossible for us
to distinguish them. On the other hand, they
frequently differ, in which case J very often has the
elder version, but often the reverse.

Thus the robust primitive version of the Hagar
story in J (chap. xvi.) is older than the lachrymose
version of E (xxi); the story of Jacob and Laban
is told more laconically and more naïvely by J than
by E; in the narrative of the birth of the children
of Jacob, J speaks with perfect frankness of the
magic effect of the mandrakes (xxx. 14 ff.), instead
of which E substitutes the operations of divine
favor (xxx. 17); in the story of Dinah, J, who
depicts Jacob's horror at the act of his sons, is more
just and more vigorous in his judgment than E,
where God himself is compelled to protect Jacob's
sons (xxxv. 5, see variant reading of RV); in the
story of Joseph the Ishmaelites of J (xxxvii. 25) are
older than the Midianites of E (xxxvii. 28) who
afterwards vanish from the account; in the testament of Jacob his wish, according to E (xlviii. 7),
to be buried beside his best loved wife is more
tender and more sentimental than his request in J
(xlvii. 29 ff.) to rest in the tomb with his ancestors;
and other similar cases might be cited.

On the other hand, E does not yet know of the
Philistines in Gerar of whom J speaks (xxi. 26); the
deception of Jacob by means of the garb of skins in
E is more naïve than that by means of the scent
of the garments in J; the many divine beings whom,
according to E, Jacob sees at Bethel are an older
conception than that of the one Jahveh in the version of J; only in J, but not yet in E, do we suddenly meet a belated Israelitising of the legend of

the covenant of Gilead (xxxi 52); in the story of
Joseph, Reuben, who had disappeared in historical
times, occupies the same position as does in J the
much better known Judah of later times; the vocabulary of E whereby he avoids the name of Jahveh
throughout Genesis, is based, as shown above (see
page 92) upon an early reminiscence which is
lacking in J; on the other hand, one cannot deny
that this absolutely consistent avoidance of the
name of Jahveh before the appearance of Moses
shows the reflexion of theological influence, which
is wholly absent in J.

These observations, which could easily be
extended, show also that there is no literary connexion between J and E; J has not copied from E,
nor E from J. If both sources occasionally agree
verbally the fact is to be explained on the basis of
a common original source.

But thirdly, the principal point is that we can see
in the manner in which the legends are brought
together in these books the evidence that we are
dealing with collections which cannot have been
completed at one given time, but developed in the
course of history. The recognition of this fact can
be derived especially from a careful observation of
the manner of J, since J furnishes us the greatest
amount of material in Genesis. The observation of
the younger critics that several sources can be distinguished in J, and especially in the story of the
beginnings, approves itself to us also; but we must
push these investigations further and deeper by sub-
stituting for a predominantly critical examination
which deals chiefly with individual books, an historical study based upon the examination of the

literary method of J and aiming to give a history of
the entire literary species.

THE JAHVIST'S SOURCES.

In J's story of the beginnings we distinguish three
sources, two of which present what were originally
independent parallel threads.   It is particularly
clear that J contained originally two parallel pedigrees of the race: beside the traditional Cainite
genealogy, a Sethite line, of which v. 29 is a fragment.   In combining the two earlier sources a third
one was also introduced, from which comes the
legend of Cain and Abel, which cannot originally
belong to a primitive time.   In the story of Abraham also we can recognise three hands: into a cycle
of legends treating the destinies of Abraham and
Lot have been introduced other elements, such as
the legend of Abraham in Egypt and the flight of
Hagar, probably from another book of legends; still
a third hand has added certain details, such as the
appeal of Abraham for Sodom.   More complicated
is the composition of the stories of Jacob: into the
cycle of Jacob, Esau and Laban have been injected
certain legends of worship; afterwards there were
added legends of the various sons of Jacob; we are
able to survey this process as a whole very well, but
are no longer able to detect the individual hands.

While the individual stories of the creation
merely stand in loose juxtaposition, some of the
Abraham stories and especially the Jacob-Esau-
Laban legends are woven into a closer unity.   This
union is still closer in the legend of Joseph.   Here
the legends of Joseph's experiences in Egypt and
with his brothers constitute a well-constructed com-

position; but here too the passage on Joseph's agrarian policy (xlvii. 13 ff.), which interrupts the connexion, shows that several different hands have been at work. Furthermore, it is quite plain that the legend of Tamar, which has no connexion with Joseph, and the "blessing of Jacob," which is a poem, not a legend, were not introduced until later.

From this survey we perceive that J is not a primary and definitive collection, but is based upon older collections and is the result of the collaboration of several hands.

The same condition is to be recognised in E, though only by slight evidences so far as Genesis is concerned, as in the present separation by the story of Ishmael (xxi. 8 ff.) of the two legends of Gerar (xx., xxi., 25 ff.) which belong together, or in the derivation of Beersheba from Abraham (xxi. 25 ff.) by the one line of narrative, from Isaac (xlvi. 1-3) by the other.

THE PROCESS OF COLLECTION.

The history of the literary collection presents, then, a very complex picture, and we may be sure that we are able to take in but a small portion of it. In olden times there may have been a whole literature of such collections, of which those preserved to us are but the fragments, just as the three synoptic gospels represent the remains of a whole gospel literature. The correctness of this view is supported by a reconstruction of the source of P, which is related to J in many respects (both containing, for instance, a story of the beginnings), but also corresponds with E at times (as in the name Paddan, attached to the characterisation of Laban as "the

Aramæan"; cp. the *Commentary*, p. 349), and also contributes in details entirely new traditions (such as the item that Abraham set out from Ur-Kasdim, the narrative of the purchase of the cave of Machpelah, and other matters).

But for the complete picture of the history of the formation of the collection the most important observation is that with which this section began: the whole process began in the stage of oral tradition. The first hands which wrote down legends probably recorded such connected stories; others then added new legends, and thus the whole body of material gradually accumulated. And thus, along with others, our collections J and E arose. J and E, then, are not individual authors, nor are they editors of older and consistent single writings, but rather they are schools of narrators. From this point of view it is a matter of comparative indifference what the individual hands contributed to the whole, because they have very little distinction and individuality, and we shall probably never ascertain with certainty. Hence we feel constrained to abstain as a matter of principle from constructing a hypothesis on the subject.

RELATION OF THE COLLECTORS TO THEIR SOURCES.

These collectors, then, are not masters, but rather servants of their subjects. We may imagine them, filled with reverence for the beautiful ancient stories and endeavoring to reproduce them as well and faithfully as they could. Fidelity was their prime quality. This explains why they accepted so many things which they but half understood and which were alien to their own taste and feeling; and why they faithfully preserved many peculiarities of individual narratives,—thus the narrative of the wooing of Rebeccah does not give the name of the city of Haran, while other passages in J are familiar with it (xxvii. 43; xxviii. 10; xxix. 4). On the other hand, we may imagine that they were secretly offended by many things in the tradition, here and there combined different versions (*Commentary*, p. 428), smoothing away the contradictions between them a little (*Commentary*, p. 332) and leaving out some older feature in order to introduce something new and different, perhaps the piece of a variant familiar to them (*Commentary*, p. 59); that they developed more clearly this motive and that, which happened to please them particularly, and even occasionally reshaped a sort of history by the combination of various traditions (*Commentary*, p. 343), and furthermore that they were influenced by the religious, ethical, and æsthetic opinions of their time to make changes here and there.

The process of remodeling the legends, which had been under way for so long, went farther in their hands. As to details, it is difficult, and for the most part impossible, to say what portion of these alterations belongs to the period of oral tradition and what portion to the collectors or to a later time. In the preceding pages many alterations have been discussed which belong to the period of written tradition. In general we are disposed to say that the oral tradition is responsible for a certain artistic inner modification, and the collectors for a more superficial alteration consisting merely of omissions and additions. Moreover, the chief point of interest is not found in this question;

it will always remain the capital matter to understand the inner reasons for the modifications.

It is also probable that some portions of considerable size were omitted or severely altered under the hands of the collectors; thus the legend of Hebron, as the promise (xviii. 10) clearly shows, presumes a continuation; some portions have been omitted from the tradition as we have it, probably by a collector; other considerable portions have been added after the whole was reduced to writing, for instance, those genealogies which are not remnants of legends, but mere outlines of ethnographic relationships; furthermore a piece such as the conversation of Abraham with God before Sodom, which by its style is of the very latest origin, and other cases of this sort. Moreover a great, primitive poem was added to the legends after they were complete (Genesis xlix).

We cannot get a complete general view of the changes made by these collections, but despite the fidelity of the collectors in details we may assume that the whole impression made by the legends has been very considerably altered by the collection and redaction they have undergone. Especially probable is it that the brilliant colors of the individual legends have been dulled in the process: what were originally prominent features of the legends lose their importance in the combination with other stories (*Commentary*, p. 161); the varying moods of the separate legends are reconciled and harmonised when they come into juxtaposition; jests, perhaps, now filled in with touches of emotion (p. 331), or combined with serious stories (*Commentary*, p. 158), cease to be recognised as mirthful;

the ecclesiastical tone of certain legends becomes the all-pervading tone of the whole to the feeling of later times. Thus the legends now make the impression of an old and originally many-colored painting that has been many times re-touched and has grown dark with age. Finally, it must be emphasised that this fidelity of the collectors is especially evident in Genesis; in the later legends, which had not such a firm hold upon the popular taste, the revision may have been more thorough-going.

RELATION OF JAHVIST TO ELOHIST.

The two schools of J and E are very closely related; their whole attitude marks them as belonging to essentially the same period. From the material which they have transmitted it is natural that the collectors should have treated with especial sympathy the latest elements, that is, particularly those which were nearest to their own time and taste. The difference between them is found first in their use of language, the most significant feature of which is that J says Jahveh before the time of Moses, while E says Elohim. Besides this there are other elements: the tribal patriarch is called "Israel" by J after the episode of Penuel, but "Jacob" by E; J calls the maid-servant "šipḥa, E calls her " 'ama," J calls the grainsack "saq," E calls it " 'amtaḥat," and so on. But, as is often the case, such a use of language is not here an evidence of a single author, but rather the mark of a district or region.

In very many cases we are unable to distinguish the two sources by the vocabulary; then the only

guide is, that the variants from the two sources
present essentially the same stories, which show
individual differences in their contents.   Thus in J
Isaac is deceived by Jacob by means of the smell of
Esau's garments, in E by the skins, a difference
which runs through a great portion of both stories.
Or, we observe that different stories have certain
pervading marks, such as, that Joseph is sold in J
by Ishmaelites to an Egyptian householder, but in
E is sold by Midianites to the eunuch Potiphar
Often evidences of this sort are far from con-
clusive; consequently we can give in such cases
nothing but conjectures as to the separation of the
sources.   And where even such indications are
lacking there is an end of all safe distinction.

In the account of the beginnings we cannot recognise the hand of E at all; it is probable that he did
not undertake to give it, but began his book with
the patriarch Abraham.   Perhaps there is in this
an expression of the opinion of the school that the
history of the beginnings was too heathenish to
deserve preservation.   Often but not always the
version of J has an older form than that of E.   J
has the most lively, objective narratives, while E,
on the other hand, has a series of sentimental, tear-
ful stories, such as the sacrifice of Isaac, the expulsion of Ishmael, and Jacob's tenderness for his
grandchildren.

Their difference is especially striking in their
conceptions of the theophany: J is characterised by
the most primitive theophanies, E, on the other
hand, by dreams and the calling of an angel out of
heaven, in a word by the least sensual sorts of
revelation.   The thought of divine Providence,

which makes even sin contribute to good ends is expressly put forth by E in the story of Joseph, but not by J. Accordingly there is reason for regarding J as older than E, as is now frequently done. Their relation to the Prophetic authors is to be treated in subsequent pages.

Inasmuch as J in the story of Joseph puts Judah in the place of Reuben, since he gives a specifically Judean version in the case of the legend of Tamar, and because he has so much to say of Abraham, who, it seems, has his real seats in Hebron and in Negeb (southward of Judah), we may agree with many recent critics in placing the home of this collection in Judah. It has been conjectured on the contrary that E has its home in Northern Israel; in fact this source speaks a great deal of Northern Israelitic localities, but yet, at the same time, much of Beersheba; furthermore, in the story of Joseph E hints once incidentally at the reign of Joseph (xxxvii. 8), though this too may be derived from the tradition. Certainly it cannot be claimed that the two collections have any strong partizan tendency in favor of the north and south kingdoms respectively.

Other characteristics of the collectors than these can scarcely be derived from Genesis. Of course, it would be easy to paint a concrete picture of J and E, if we venture to attribute to them whatever is to be found in their books. But this is forbidden by the very character of these men as collectors.[1]

---

[1] If the reader cannot be satisfied with the little that we have given, he must at least be very much more cautious than, for instance, such a writer as Holzinger on the Hexateuch.

THE AGE OF THE JAHVIST AND ELOHIST SCHOOLS.

The question of the absolute age of J and E is exceedingly difficult. We, who believe that we have here to deal with a gradual codification of ancient traditions, are constrained to resolve this question into a number of subordinate questions: When did these traditions arise? When did they become known in Israel? When did they receive essentially their present form? When were they written down? That is to say, our task is not to fix a single definite date; but we are to make a chronological scale for a long process. But this is a very difficult problem, for intellectual processes are very difficult in general to fix chronologically; and there is the further difficulty that blocks us in general with all such questions about the Old Testament, that we know too little about ancient Israel in order to warrant positive conclusions in the present case. Very many of the chronological conjectures of literary criticism, in so far as they are based only upon the study of the history of religion, are more or less unsafe.

The origin of many of the legends lies in what is for Israel a prehistoric age. Even the laconic style of the legends is primitive; the stories of the "Judges" are already in a more detailed style. After the entrance of Israel into Canaan foreign themes come in in streams. Very many of the legends presuppose the possession of the land and a knowledge of its localities. Among the Israelitish subjects, the genealogy of the twelve sons of Jacob does not correspond with the seats of the tribes in Canaan, and must, therefore, represent older relations. The latest of the Israelitish legends of Genesis that we know treat the retirement of Reuben, the origin of the families of Judah and the assault upon Shechem, that is, events from the earlier portion of the period of the "Judges." In the later portion of this period the poetic treatment of races as individuals was no longer current: by this time new legends of the patriarchs had ceased to be formed.

The period of the formation of legends of the patriarchs is, then, closed with this date (about 1200). The correctness of this estimate is confirmed by other considerations: the sanctuary at Jerusalem, so famous in the time of kings, is not referred to in the legends of the patriarchs; on the contrary the establishment of this sanctuary is placed by the legends of worship in the time of David (2 Sam. xxiv.). The reign of Saul, the conflict of Saul with David, the united kingdom under David and Solomon, the separation of the two kingdoms and the war between them,—we hear no echoes of all this in the older legends; a clear proof that no new legends of the patriarchs were being formed at that time. At what time the legends of Moses, Joshua and others originated is a question for discussion elsewhere.

RE-MODELING OF THE LEGENDS.

The period of the formation of the legends is followed by one of re-modeling. This is essentially the age of the earlier kings. That is probably the time when Israel was again gathered together from its separation into different tribes and districts to one united people, the time when the various distinct traditions grew together into a common body

of national legends.   The great growth which Israel
experienced under the first kings probably yielded
it the moral force to lay claim to the foreign tales
and give them a national application.   At this time
the Jacob-Esau legend received its interpretation
referring to Israel and Edom: Israel has in the
meantime subjected Edom, the event occurring
under David, and Judah retaining her possession
until about 840.   Meanwhile Ephraim has out-
stripped Manasseh, probably in the beginning of
the period of the kings.   In the legend of Joseph
there occurs an allusion to the dominion of Joseph
(xxxvii. 8, E), which, however, found its way into
the legend at some later time.   The dreadful Syrian
wars, which begin about the year 900, are not yet
mentioned in the Jacob-Laban legend, but only
occasional border forays.   The city of Asshur,
which was the capital until 1300, has passed from the
memory of the Hebrew tradition; but Nineveh (x.
11), the capital from about 1000 on, seems to be
known to it.   Accordingly we may at least assume
that by 900 B.C. the legends were essentially, so far
as the course of the narrative goes, as we now read
them.

As for allusions to political occurrences later than
900, we have only a reference to the rebellion of
Edom (about 840), which, however, is plainly an
addition to the legend (xxvii. 40*b*).   The other
cases that are cited are inconclusive: the reference
to the Assyrian cities (x. 11 ff.) does not prove
that these passages come from the "Assyrian"
period, for Assyria had certainly been known to the
Israelites for a long time; just as little does the
mention of Kelah warrant a conclusion, for the

city was restored in 870, though it had been the capital since about 1300 (in both of these points I differ from the conclusions of Cornill, *Einleitung in das Alte Testament*,³ p. 46). According to Lagarde, *Mitteilungen*, III., p. 226 ff., the Egyptian names in Genesis xli. bring us down into the seventh century; but this is by no means positive, for the names which were frequently heard at that time had certainly been known in earlier times.

But even though no new political references crept into the legends after about 900, and though they have remained unchanged in their essentials from this time on, they may nevertheless have undergone many internal alterations. This suggests a comparison with a piece like Genesis xlix.: this piece, coming from the time of David, harmonises in tone with the oldest legends. Hence we may assume another considerable period during which the religious and moral changes in the legends above mentioned were taking place. This period lasts over into that of the collection of the legends and is closed by it.

RELATION OF THE COLLECTIONS TO THE PROPHETS.

When did the collection of the legends take place? This question is particularly difficult, for we have only internal data for its solution, and we can establish these in their turn only after establishing the date of the sources. So unfortunately we are moving here in the familiar circle, and with no present prospect of getting out of it. Investigators must consider this before making unqualified declarations on the subject. Furthermore it is to be borne in mind that not even these collections were completed all at once, but grew into shape through a process which lasted no one can say how many decades or centuries. The real question in fixing the date of the sources is the relation of the two to the authors of the "Prophets." Now there are, to be sure, many things in Genesis that suggest a relation with these Prophets, but the assumption of many modern critics that this relation must be due to some direct influence of the Prophetic writers is very doubtful in many cases; we do not know the religion of Israel sufficiently well to be able to declare that certain thoughts and sentiments were first brought to light by the very Prophets whose writings we possess (all later than Amos): the earnestness with which the legend of the Deluge speaks of the universal sinfulness of mankind, and the glorification of the faith of Abraham are not specifically "Prophetic." The hostility of the collectors to the images of Jahveh and to the Asherim (sacred poles), of which they never speak, to the Massëbâh (obelisks), which J passes over but E still mentions, to the "golden calf" which is regarded by the legend according to E (Exodus xxxii.) as sinful, as well as to the teraphim, which the Jacob-Laban legend wittily ridicules (xxxi. 30 f.),—all of this may easily be independent of "Prophetic" influence. Sentiments of this nature may well have existed in Israel long before the "Prophets," indeed we must assume their existence in order to account for the appearance of the "Prophets."

True, E calls Abraham a *nabi* (prophet), xx. 7; that is to say, he lived at a time when "Prophet" and "man of God" were identical; but the guild

of the Nᵉbiim was flourishing long before the time
of Amos, and in Hosea also, xii. 14, Moses is
called a "Prophet." Accordingly there is nothing
in the way of regarding E and J both as on the
whole "pre-Prophetic." This conclusion is supported by a number of considerations: the Prophetic
authors are characterised by their predictions of
the destruction of Israel, by their polemic against
alien gods and against the high places of Israel,
and by their rejection of sacrifices and ceremonials.
These very characteristic features of the "Prophets"
are absent in J and E in Genesis, J has no notion
of other gods at all except Jahveh, and Jacob's
abolition of alien gods for the sake of a sacred
ceremony in honor of Jahveh, xxxv. 4 in the tradition of E, does not sound like a "Prophetic"
utterance. Of an opposition to strange gods there
is never any talk, at least not in Genesis.

And while these collections contain nothing that
is characteristically Prophetic, they have on the
other hand much that must needs have been exceedingly offensive to the Prophets: they have, for
instance, an especially favorable attitude toward
the sacred places which the Prophets assail so bit-
terly; they maintain toward the primitive religion and morality a simple leniency which is the
very opposite of the fearful accusations of the
Prophets.

We can see from the Prophetic redaction of the
historical books what was the attitude of the legitimate pupils of the Prophets toward ancient tradition: they would certainly not have cultivated the
popular legends, which contained so much that was
heathen, but rather have obliterated them.

In view of these considerations we must conclude that the collections took shape in all essentials before the period of great Prophetic writings, and that the touches of the spirit of this movement in J and E but show that the thoughts of the Prophets were in many a man's mind long before the time of Amos. This conclusion is supported by a number of other considerations: the legend of the exodus of Abraham, which glorifies his faith, presumes on the other hand the most flourishing prosperity of Israel, and accordingly comes most surely from the time before the great incursion of the Assyrians. And pieces which from the point of view of the history of legends are so late as chapter 15, or as the story of the birth of the sons of Jacob, contain, on the other hand, very ancient religious motives.

But this does not exclude the possibility that certain of the very latest portions of the collections are in the true sense "Prophetic." Thus Abraham's conversation with God before Sodom is in its content the treatment of a religious problem, but in form it is an imitation of the Prophetic "expostulation" with God. Joshua's farewell (Joshua xxiv.) with its unconcealed distrust of Israel's fidelity is also in form an imitation of the Prophetic sermon. In the succeeding books, especially the portions due to E, there is probably more of the same character, but in Genesis the instances are rare.

Accordingly we may locate both collections before the appearance of the great Prophets, J perhaps in the ninth century and E in the first half of the eighth; but it must be emphasized that such dates are after all very uncertain.

THE JEHOVIST REDACTOR.

The two collections were united later by an editor designated as R^{JE}, whom, following Wellhausen's example, we shall call the "Jehovist." This union of the two older sources took place before the addition of the later book of legends to be referred to as P. We may place this collector somewhere near the end of the kingdom of Judah. R^{JE} manifests in Genesis the most extraordinary conservatism and reverence; he has expended a great amount of keenness in trying to retain both sources so far as possible and to establish the utmost possible harmony between them. In general he probably took the more detailed source for his basis, in the story of Abraham J. He himself appears with his own language very little in Genesis. We recognise his pen with certainty in a few brief additions which are intended to harmonise the variants of J and E, but of which there are relatively few: xvi. 9 f.; xxviii. 21$_b$, and further in xxxi. 49 ff.; xxxix. 1; xli. 50; xlv. 19; xlvi. 1; l. 11; and several points in xxxiv; but the most of these instances are trifles.

Furthermore, there are certain, mostly rather brief, additions, which we may locate in this period and probably attribute to this redactor or to his contemporaries. Some of them merely run over and deepen the delicate lines of the original text: xviii. 17-19; xx. 18; xxii. 15-18; some are priestly elaborations of profane narratives: xiii. 14-17; xxxii. 10-13; the most of them are speeches attributed to God; xiii. 14-17; xvi. 9 and 10; xviii. 17-19; xxii. 15-18; xxvi. 3$_b$-5, 24, 25a; xxviii. 14; xlvi. 3 β (xxxii. 10-13; l. 24γ); which is characteristic for

these latest additions, which profess only to give
thoughts and not stories, speeches containing especially solemn promises for Israel: that it was to
become a mighty nation and take possession of "all
these lands." Incidentally all the people are
enumerated which Israel is to conquer: xv. 19-21; x.
16-18. These additions come from the period
when the great world crises were threatening the
existence of Israel, and when the faith of the people
was clinging to these promises, that is to say, probably from the Chaldæan period. Here and there
we meet a trace of "Deuteronomistic" style: xviii.
17-19; xxvi. 3b-5.

VI.

PRIESTLY CODEX AND FINAL REDACTION.

VI.

PRIESTLY CODEX AND FINAL REDACTION.

BESIDES those already treated we find evidence of another separate stream of tradition. This source is so distinct from the other sources both in style and spirit that in the great majority of cases it can be separated from them to the very letter. This collection also is not limited to Genesis; on the contrary, the legends of the beginnings and of the patriarchs are to it merely a brief preparation for the capital matter, which is the legislation of Moses. The Priestly Codex is of special importance for us because the entire discussion of the Old Testament has hitherto turned essentially upon its data. It is Wellhausen's immortal merit (*Prolegomena*,[4] p. 299 ff.) to have recognised the true character of this source, which had previously been considered the oldest, to have demonstrated thus the incorrectness of the entire general view of the Old Testament, and thus to have prepared the field for a living and truly historical understanding of the history of the religion of Israel.

The style of P is extremely peculiar, exceedingly detailed and aiming at legal clearness and minuteness, having always the same expressions and formulæ, with precise definitions and monotonous set phrases with consistently employed outlines which

lack substance, with genealogies and with titles
over every chapter. It is the tone of prosaic
pedantry, often indeed the very style of the legal
document (for instance xi. 11; and xxiii. 17, 18);
occasionally, however, it is not without a certain
solemn dignity (especially in Genesis i. and elsewhere also, cp. the scene xlvii. 7-11). One must
really read the whole material of P consecutively in
order to appreciate the dryness and monotony of
this remarkable book. The author is evidently
painfully exact and exemplary in his love of order,
but appreciation of poetry was denied him as to
many another scholar.

The selection of material both in large and in
small matters is highly characteristic in P. The
only stories of any length which he gives us are those
of the Creation and the Deluge, of God's appearance to Abraham and of the purchase of the cave at
Machpelah; all else is details and genealogies.
From by far the greatest number of narratives he
found use only for separate and disconnected observations. One has only to compare the ancient
variegated and poetic legends and the scanty reports
which P gives of them, in order to learn where his
interests lie: he does not purpose to furnish a poetic
narrative, as those of old had done, but only to
arrive at the facts. This is why he was unable to
use the many individual traits contained in the old
legends, but merely took from them a very few
facts. He ignored the sentiments of the legends,
he did not see the personal life of the patriarchs;
their figures, once so concrete, have become mere
pale types when seen through his medium. In
times of old many of these legends had been located

in definite places, thereby gaining life and color; P
has forgotten all but two places: the cave of Machpelah, where the patriarchs dwelt and lie buried, and
Bethél, where God revealed himself to Jacob.   On
the other hand, he has a great predilection for
genealogies, which, as we have seen, were the latest
elements to be contributed to the accumulation of
the legend, and which are in their very nature
unconcrete and unpoetical.   A very large portion
of P's share in Genesis is genealogy and nothing
more.

Even those narratives which are told by P at
length manifest this same lack of color.   They are
narratives that are not really stories.   The account
of the purchase of the cave of Machpelah might
have been nothing but an incidental remark in one
of the older story-tellers; P has spun it out at length
because he wanted to establish as beyond all doubt
the fact that the cave really belonged to the patriarchs
and was an ancestral sepulcher.   But he had not the
poetic power necessary to shape the account into a
story.   In the great affairs of state which P gives
instead of the old stories, story-telling has ceased,
there is only talking and negotiating (Wellhausen).
Even the accounts of the Creation, the Deluge
and the Covenant with Abraham manifest a wide
contrast with the vivid colors of the older legends;
they lack greatly in the concrete elements of a
story.   Instead of this P gives in them something
else, something altogether alien to the spirit of the
early legend, to wit, legal ordinances, and these in
circumstantial detail.   Another characteristic of P
is his pronounced liking for outlines; this order-lov-
ing man has ensnared the gay legends of the olden

time in his gray outlines, and there they have lost all their poetic freshness: take as an illustration the genealogy of Adam and Seth. Even the stories of the patriarchs have been caged by P in an outline.

IMPORTANCE ATTACHED TO CHRONOLOGY.

Furthermore P attaches to the legends a detailed chronology, which plays a great rôle in his account, but is absolutely out of keeping with the simplicity of the old legends. Chronology belongs by its very nature to history, not to legend. Where historical narrative and legend exist as living literary species, they are recognised as distinct, even though unconsciously. This confusion of the two species in P shows that in his time the natural appreciation for both history and legend had been lost. Accordingly it is not strange that the chronology of P displays everywhere the most absurd oddities when injected into the old legends: as a result, Sarah is still at sixty-five a beautiful woman whom the Egyptians seek to capture, and Ishmael is carried on his mother's shoulder after he is a youth of sixteen.

There has been added a great division of the world's history into periods, which P forces upon the whole matter of his account. He recognises four periods: from the creation to Noah, from Noah to Abraham, from Abraham to Moses, and from Moses on. Each of these periods begins with a theophany, and twice a new name for God is introduced. He who is Elohim at the creation is El Shaddai in connexion with Abraham and Jahveh to Moses. At the establishment of the Covenant certain divine ordinances are proclaimed:

first, that men and beasts are to eat only herbs, and then, after the Deluge, that flesh may be eaten but no men be slain, and then, especially for Abraham, that he and his descendants shall circumcise themselves; finally, the Mosaic law.

In connexion with these, certain definite divine promises are made and signs of the Covenant given. What we find in this is the product of a great and universal mind, the beginning of a universal history in the grand style, and indeed P shows a genuinely scientific mind in other points: consider, for instance, his precision in the order of creation in Genesis i. and his definitions there. But the material of the legends which this grandiose universal history uses stands in very strong contrast with the history itself: the signs of the Covenant are a rainbow, circumcision and the Sabbath, a very remarkable list! And how remote is this spirit of universal history, which even undertakes to estimate the duration of the entire age of the world, from the spirit of the old legend, which originally consists of only a single story that is never able to rise to the height of such general observations: in J, for instance, we hear nothing of the relation of Abraham's religion to that of his fathers and his tribal kinsmen.

THE RELIGIOUS VIEWS OF THE PRIESTLY CODEX.

Furthermore, we cannot deny that this reflexion of P's, that Jahveh first revealed himself in quite a general form as "God," and then in a concreter form as El Shaddai, and only at the last under his real name, is, after all, very childish: the real history of religion does not begin with the general and then pass to the concrete, but on the contrary, it begins with the very most concrete conceptions, and only slowly and gradually do men learn to comprehend what is abstract.

It is characteristic of the religion of the author P that he says almost nothing about the personal piety of the patriarchs; he regards only the objective as important in religion. For instance, he says nothing about Abraham's obedience on faith; indeed does not hesitate to report that Abraham laughed at God's promise (xvii. 17). The religion that he knows consists in the prescription of ceremonies; he regards it of importance that the Sabbath shall be observed, that circumcision shall be practised, that certain things shall be eaten and others not. In such matters he is very scrupulous. He abstains, evidently with deliberation, from telling that the patriarchs offered sacrifice in any certain place, and this evidently for the reason that these places were regarded as heathenish in his time. Similarly, in his account of the Deluge, he does not distinguish the clean and the unclean beasts. It is his opinion that established worship and the distinction of clean and unclean were not introduced until the time of Moses.

But in this we hear the voice of a priest of Jerusalem, whose theory is that the worship at his sanctuary is the only legitimate worship and the continuation of the worship instituted by Moses. The Israelitish theocracy—this, in modern phrase, is the foundation thought of his work—is the purpose of the world. God created the world in order that his ordinances and commandments might be observed in the temple at Jerusalem.

The theophanies of P are characterised by their inconcreteness; he tells only that God appeared, spoke, and again ascended, and leaves out everything else. In this, then, he follows the style of the latest additions to JE, which also contain such speeches attributed to God without any introduction. It is evident that in this there is expressed a religious hesitation on the part of P to involve the supermundane God with the things of this world; it seems as though he suspected the heathen origin of these theophanies. At the same time we perceive what his positive interest is: he cares for the content of the divine revelation, but not for its "How." Moreover, it is no accident that he conceives of these speeches of God as "covenant-making": evidently he has in mind this originally legal form. This union of the priest, the scholar, and the distinctive lawyer, which seems to us perhaps remarkable at first, is after all quite natural: among many ancient races the priesthood was the guardian of learning and especially of the law. And thus it surely was in Israel too, where from primitive times the priests were accustomed to settle difficult disputes. P developed his style in the writing of contracts—this is quite evident in many places.

But it is especially characteristic of P that he no longer refers to the sacred symbols, which had once possessed such great importance for the ancient religion, as may be seen particularly in the legends of the patriarchs; in him we no longer find a reference to the monuments, the trees and groves, and the springs at which, according to the ancient legends, the divinity appeared. P has expunged all such matter from the legend, evidently because

he considered it heathenish. Here we see plainly
the after-effects of the fearful polemics of the
Prophets: it is the same spirit which branded the
ancient sacred place of Bethel as heathen (in the
"reform" of Josiah) and which here rejects from the
ancient legends everything that smacks of heathen-
ism to these children of a later time.

This much, then, is certain, that the conceptions
of God in P are loftier and more advanced than
those of the old legends; and yet P is far below
these older authors, who had not made the acquaintance of the sacerdotalism of Jerusalem, but who did
know what piety is. Just as P purified the religion
of the patriarchs, so did he also purge their
morality. Here, too, P adds the last word to a
development which we have followed up in J and E.
The old legends of the patriarchs, being an expression of the most primitive life of the people, contained a great deal that those of a later time could
not but regard as wrong and sinful, if they were
quite honest about it.

And yet, the belief of the time was that the
patriarchs were models of piety and virtue. What
pains had been taken to eliminate at least the most
offensive things in this line so far as possible!
When it comes to P at last, he makes a clean sweep:
he simply omits altogether what is offensive (for
instance, the quarrel of the shepherds of Abraham
and Lot, Lot's selfishness, the exile of Ishmael,
Jacob's deceptions); he even goes to the length of
maintaining the precise contrary to the tradition:
Ishmael and Isaac together peacefully buried their
father (xxv. 9), and so did Jacob and Esau (xxxv.
29). Facts which cannot be obliterated receive a

different motivation: thus he explains Isaac's blessing of Jacob as a result of Esau's sinful mixed marriages (xxvi. 34 f.; xxviii. 1 ff.), and he lays the
crime against Joseph at the door of the sons of
Bilhah and Zilpah (xxxvii. 2).

From all of this it appears clear that P dealt very
arbitrarily with the tradition as it came down to him.
He dropped old versions or changed them at pleasure; mere incidents he spun out to complete
stories, and from whole stories he adopted only incidents; he mingled the motives of various legends,
declaring, for instance, that the blessing received by
Jacob from Isaac was the blessing of Abraham,
which had been entirely foreign to the thought of
the old story-tellers (xxviii. 4; other instances may
be found pp. 237, 247, 350 of the *Commentary*);
from the stories of the old tradition, which stood in
loose juxtaposition, he formed a continuous narrative with close connexion,—this, too, a mark of
the latest period. In place of the legends he placed
his chapters with regular headings!

This narrator, then, has no conception of the
fidelity of the older authors; he probably had an
impression that it was necessary to lay on vigorously
in order to erect a structure worthy of God. The
older authors, J and E, were really not authors, but
merely collectors, while P is a genuine author; the
former merely accumulated the stone left to them
in a loose heap; but P erected a symmetrical structure in accordance with his own taste. And yet we
should be wrong if we should assume that he
deliberately invented his allegations in Genesis;
tradition was too strong to permit even him to do
this. On the contrary, he simply worked over the

material, though very vigorously indeed; we can
often recognise by details how he followed his
source in the general outline of events when no personal interest of his own was involved (see p. 139 of
the *Commentary*). But this source, at least for
Genesis, was neither J nor E but one related to
them.

THE AGE OF THE PRIESTLY CODEX.

After this portrayal of the situation the age of P
is evident. It belongs by every evidence at the
close of the whole history of the tradition, and certainly separated by a great gap from J and E: the
living stream of legend from which J and E, the old
collectors, had dipped, must by that time have run
dry, if it had become possible for P to abuse it in
this fashion for the construction of his history.
And in the meanwhile a great intellectual revolution
must have taken place,—a revolution which had
created something altogether new in the place of
the old nationality represented in the legends.

P is the documentary witness of a time which was
consciously moving away from the old traditions,
and which believed it necessary to lay the foundations of religion in a way differing from that of the
fathers. And in P we have revealed the nature of
this new element which had then assumed sway,—it
is the spirit of the learned priest that we here find
expressed. Furthermore, this also is clear to us
from the whole manner of P, and particularly from
his formal language, that we have not here the work
of an individual with a special tendency, but of a
whole group whose convictions he expresses. P's
work is nothing more nor less than an official
utterance.

It is the priesthood of Jerusalem with which the document P originated. Hence the applicableness of the designation "Priestly Codex." Wellhausen has revealed to us the time to which this spirit belonged. This is the epoch following the great catastrophe to the people and the state of Judah, when the people, overwhelmed by the tremendous impression of their measureless misfortune, recognised that their fathers had sinned, and that a great religious reformation was necessary. Only in connexion with this period can we comprehend P with his grandiose want of respect for what had been the most sacred traditions of his people. We know also well enough that it was the priesthood alone in that day which held its own and kept the people together after all other authorities had worn themselves out or perished: after its restoration the congregation of Judah was under the dominion of priests.

In keeping with this period also is the remarkably developed historical scholarship of P. The older epoch had produced excellent story-tellers, but no learned historians; while in this period of exile Judæan historiography had lost its naïve innocence. Under the powerful influence of the superior Babylonian civilisation Judaism also had acquired a taste for precise records of numbers and measures. It now grew accustomed to employ great care in statistical records: genealogical tables were copied, archives were searched for authentic documents, chronological computations were undertaken, and even universal history was cultivated after the Babylonian model. In Ezra and Nehemiah and Chronicles we see the same historical scholarship as in P, and in Ezekiel, Haggai, and Zechariah the same high value placed upon exact chronology. The reckoning of the months also, which is found in P, was learned by the Jews at this time, and probably from Babylonia. The progress represented by this learned spirit as compared with the simplicity of former times is undeniable, even though the products of this learning often fail to appeal to us. It is probably characteristic of the beginnings of "universal history" that such first great historical constructions as we have in P deal largely with mythical or legendary materials, and are consequently inadequate according to our modern notions. In this respect P may be compared to Berosus.

The emphasis laid by P upon the Sabbath, the prohibition of bloodshed and circumcision, is also comprehensible to us in the light of this period: the epoch in which everything depended on the willingness of the individual emphasised the religious commandments which applied to the individual. Indeed it may be said, that the piety of the patriarchs, who are always represented as *gerim* (strangers), and who have to get along without sacrifices and formal ceremonies, is a reflexion of the piety of the exile, when those who lived in the foreign land had neither temples nor sacrifices.

P's religious criticism of mixed marriages also, especially those with Canaanitish women, whereby the blessing of Abraham was forfeited (xxviii. 1-9) connect with the same time, when the Jews, living in the Dispersion, had no more zealous desire than to keep their blood and their religion pure.

Much more characteristic than these evidences taken from Genesis are the others derived from the legal sections of the following books. Finally there is to be added to all these arguments the late origin of the style of P[1]. And in accordance with this the fixing of the date of P as coming from the time of the exile is one of the surest results of criticism.

We need not attempt to determine here in just what century P wrote; but this much may be said, that the Law-book of Ezra, in the opinion of many scholars, upon which the congregation took the oath in 444, and in the composition of which Ezra was in some way involved, was P. Hence we may place the composition of the book in the period from 500 to 444. P, too, was not completed all at once, though this is hardly a matter of importance so far as Genesis goes

THE FINAL REDACTOR.

The final redactor, who combined the older work of JE and P, and designated as R[JEP], probably belongs, therefore, to the time after Ezra, and surely before the time of the separation of the Samaritan congregation, which carried the complete Pentateuch along with it—though we are unable, indeed, to give the exact date of this event. The fact that such a combination of the older and the later collections was necessary shows us that the old legends had been planted too deep in the popular heart to be supplanted by the new spirit.

Great historical storms had in the meantime desecrated the old sacred places; the whole past

---

[1] Wellhausen, *Prologomena*, p. 393, ff. Ryssel, *De elohistæ pentateuchici sermone*, 1878. Giesebrecht, *ZAW*, 1881, p. 177 ff. Driver, *Journal of Philology*, 1882, p. 201 ff.

seemed to the men of the new time to be sinful.
And yet the old legends which glorified these places
and which gave such a naïve reflexion of the olden
time, could not be destroyed. The attempt of P to
supplant the older tradition had proven a failure;
accordingly a reverent hand produced a combination of JE and P.

This last collection was prepared with extraordinary fidelity, especially toward P; its author aimed
if possible not to lose a single grain of P's work.
We shall not blame him for preferring P to JE, for
P never ceased to dominate Jewish taste. Especially notable is the fact that the redactor applied
the chronology of P as a framework for the narratives
of J and E. In Genesis there are a very few features
which we can trace with more or less certainty to
his hand: such are a few harmonising comments or
elaborations like x. 24; xv. 7, 8, 15; xxvii. 46;
xxxv. 13, 14; and further some retouching in vi. 7;
vii. 7, 22, 23; and also vii. 3$_a$, 8, 9; and finally the
distinction between Abram and Abraham, Sarai and
Sarah, which is also found in J and E, and some
other matters.

We have now covered the activities of all the
various redactors of Genesis. But in smaller details
the work on the text (Diaskeuase) continues for a
long time. Smaller alterations are to be found in
xxxiv. and in the numbers of the genealogies, in
which the Jewish and the Samaritan text, and the
Greek translation differ. More considerable alterations were made in xxxvi. and xlvi. 8-27; while the
last large interpolation is the narrative of Abraham's victory over the four kings, a legend from
very late times, and of "midrash" character.

SUMMARY.

Thus Genesis has been compounded from very many sources. And in the last state we have described it has remained. In this form the old legends have exercised an incalculable influence upon all succeeding generations. We may perhaps regret that the last great genius who might have created out of the separate stories a great whole, a real "Israelitic national epic," never came. Israel produced no Homer. But this is fortunate for our investigation; for just because the individual portions have been left side by side and in the main unblended it is possible for us to make out the history of the entire process. For this reason students of the legend should apply themselves to the investigation of Genesis, which has not been customary hitherto; while theologians should learn that Genesis is not to be understood without the aid of the proper methods for the study of legends.

HOW GENESIS CAME TO BE ATTRIBUTED TO MOSES.

One word more, in closing, as to how Genesis has obtained the undeserved honor of being regarded as a work of Moses. From primitive times there existed a tradition in Israel that the divine ordinances regarding worship, law and morality, as proclaimed by the mouth of the priests, were derived from Moses. When, then, these ordinances, which had originally circulated orally, were written down in larger or smaller works, it was natural that they passed under the name of Moses Now our Pentateuch consists, in addition to the collections of legends, of such books of law from various periods and of very diverse spirit. And because

the legends also, from the time of the Exodus, have
to do chiefly with Moses, it was very easy to combine both legends and laws ir one single book.
Thus it happened that Genesis has become the first
part of a work whose follcwing parts tell chiefly of
Moses and contain many laws that claim to come
from Moses. But in its contents Genesis has no
connexion with Moses. These narratives, among
them so many of a humorous, an artistic, or a sentimental character, are very remote from the spirit of
such a strenuous and wrathful Titan as Moses,
according to the tradition, must have been.

INDEX.

INDEX.

161